BRAIN BASED THERAPY FOR ANXIETY

A Workbook for Clinicians and Clients

JOHN B. ARDEN PH.D.

Author of The Brain Based Therapy for OCD:
A workbook for Clinicians and Clients

PESI
Publishing
& Media
www.pesipublishing.com

Copyright © 2014 by John B. Arden Ph.D.
Published by
PESI Publishing & Media
PESI, Inc
3839 White Ave
Eau Claire, WI 54703

Printed in the United States of America

ISBN: 978-1-936-12800-6

All rights reserved. No part of this book may be reproduced or transmitted in any form or by any means, electronic or mechanical, including photo copying, recording, or by any information storage and retrieval system without the written permission from the author (except for the inclusion of brief quotations in a review).

PESI
Publishing
& Media
www.pesipublishing.com

Contents

Introduction

If you are plagued by anxiety, you are not alone. Anxiety disorders are more common in the United States than any other psychological problem, including depression. Some estimates indicate that one-fifth of all adults have experienced an anxiety disorder at some point in their lives.

We live in a stress-filled world. Terrorism, financial and job pressures, and the wars in Iraq and Afghanistan have all contributed to an underlying sense of anxiety in our day-to-day lives. Although most of us find ways to deal with that anxiety, some people experience it in the extreme and can, as a result, develop anxiety disorders.

Living with an anxiety disorder can be a challenge. It can make getting through the day and enjoying your life difficult. An anxiety disorder can put your life in *dis*order.

The good news is that you can bring your anxiety disorder under control. Just as your body has the ability to heal wounds, so can your brain. Your brain has the capacity to change through a process known as *neuroplasticity,* which means rewiring your brain.

This workbook will help you discover how to do just that. It contains the step-by-step lessons that I teach in my Mastering Anxiety class. You'll learn:

- how anxiety develops
- the types of anxiety
- how your brain works and how to rewire it
- what you can do to make your brain more capable of rewiring
- which foods and nutritional supplements create the right biochemistry to help your brain make you calmer
- how to restructure your thinking, so that you can make your anxiety work *for* you, instead of against you
- how to avoid *avoidance* and maximize *exposure* (you'll find out more about these in chapter 8)
- how to keep from overreacting to the physical sensations associated with anxiety
- how to prevent relapse

In the following chapters, you'll discover the practices that can help you overcome panic disorder, phobia, and generalized anxiety. These practices are what I call "brain-based" and "evidence-based." Brain-based practices help you change how you think. Because your brain is central to everything you do and feel, when you rewire your brain, you can put anxiety behind you. Evidence-based practices are techniques that are known to help overcome anxiety. After performing hundreds of studies on treating anxiety disorders, psychologists have found that some techniques work and some do not. You are going to learn the ones that work. These evidence-based practices form the basis of two books I have written for professional therapists on brain-based therapy.

In this book, you'll discover how to heal your anxiety from a *biopsychosocial* perspective—that is, biologically, psychologically, and socially. A biopsychosocial approach is comprehensive because anxiety encompasses biological (your brain and the rest of your body), psychological (thinking and feeling), and social (social and cultural contexts) aspects. By following the practices in this book, you can physically change your brain and body, change the way you think to help you change the way you feel, and change the way you approach social situations. You'll learn how to rewire your brain and alter the way your body functions. You'll learn to restructure your thoughts, so that your emotions can follow their lead. You'll also learn to use the social world around you to enhance your comfort level.

You live in a social world with culturally defined methods of dealing with problems, including anxiety. Some of these are unhelpful and lead to misunderstandings. You'll learn which socially sanctioned methods to discard and which ones to embrace.

What this book will *not* cover is the use of medications to treat anxiety disorders. My position with respect to medication is that less is more. Although I am not fundamentally against the use of medications, I find that most people can heal their anxiety without them. Antianxiety medications, such as Ativan and Valium, can impede your ability to heal your anxiety in the long term and can contribute to a wide range of negative side effects, such as depression, sleep problems, and addiction. Selective Serotonin Reuptake Inhibitors (SSRIs), such as Paxil and Prozac, have been found to have anti-anxiety effects, but they also come with side effects. If you want your gains to be permanent, don't rely on medications. They are only useful when you use them. Try the methods described in this book before considering medications.

This book will also not cover post-traumatic stress disorder (PTSD) or obsessive-compulsive disorder (OCD). If you have PTSD or OCD, you'll want to refer to one of my other books: *Conquering Post-Traumatic Stress Disorder* (with Dr. Victoria Beckner) and *The Heal-Your-OCD Workbook* (with Dr. Daniel Dal Corso).

Finally, this is not just a book *about* anxiety. It is a book on *how to heal* your anxiety. As you read through it, you'll not only *learn* how to overcome excessive anxiety, but you'll also be *practicing* methods to overcome it, through a series of exercises. With practice and the techniques you learn in the book, you, too, can live a life free of anxiety disorders.

Chapter 1
What Is Anxiety and What Causes It?

Everyone experiences anxiety once in a while—when the car breaks down on the way to a job interview, for example, or when you're standing on the high-diving board and the water looks a *long* way down. Anxiety is a fact of life. In fact, *some* anxiety is necessary. You need a little anxiety to get to work on time or to get to the grocery store before it closes. If you didn't have anxiety, you wouldn't know to get out of the way when you see a truck bearing down on you in the street.

Anxiety can be a bad thing, however, if you worry that your boss doesn't like you, even though you have no realistic evidence that he does not, or if you feel panic when there are "too many" people in the grocery store, or if you avoid crossing streets, because you never know when a truck is going to come out of nowhere. Anxiety becomes a problem when it gets turned on too high.

Feeling constant tension and worry makes each day trying at best and a walking nightmare at worst. And when you're extremely fearful about a situation—meeting new people, for instance—your life becomes severely limited. You can feel like you're walking through a minefield when you're plagued by panic attacks, because you never know when one might occur. When anxiety becomes extreme, it's considered an *anxiety disorder.* But an anxiety disorder doesn't have to be permanent.

How Jake and Tom Experience Anxiety

Jake and Tom were both scheduled to take a seminar on a new computer program. Jake was excited about the opportunity to get out of the office and meet new people. Although he was a little anxious about whether he was going to be able to learn the entire system, he was eager to give it a try.

Tom was reluctant to go to the seminar. He tried to get out of it by saying he had too much work to do at the office. Secretly, he feared having to meet new people and was particularly afraid of being asked to speak. He even thought of quitting his job, so that he would not have to go to the seminar, but decided against it because it would mean going to job interviews, which he feared more than the seminar. As Tom drove to the building in which the seminar was being held, his heart began to pound, his breathing became shallow, and he started sweating profusely. As he stepped out of the car, his thoughts raced by so fast, he couldn't decide what to do. Should he go to the hospital, or should he sit back down in his car and hope this nightmare didn't kill him?

When Jake arrived, he anxiously looked Tom over and asked, "Are you okay? Should I call the paramedics?"

Tom nodded yes. Jake dialed 911, then anxiously turned to Tom. "Is it your heart?" Tom looked horrified and again nodded yes. Jake paced nervously, hoping that the ambulance would arrive before Tom died.

Which of these two men had anxiety? Both did. But Jake's anxiety was adaptive. It helped him spring into action to help a man in distress.

Tom's anxiety was maladaptive. In fact, he was having a panic attack. Tom's anxiety was a problem, because he became paralyzed by it. Tom is an example of someone with an anxiety disorder.

SYMPTOMS OF ANXIETY DISORDERS

If you suffer from an anxiety disorder, you're probably already familiar with at least some of the symptoms: breathlessness, racing heartbeat, dizziness, and a fear of choking, in the case of panic disorder; irritability, difficulty concentrating, restlessness, and constant worry, in the case of generalized anxiety disorder; or intense fear of a particular situation, object, or environment, such as grocery stores, in the case of phobia. You might not experience all the symptoms common to a specific disorder, and you might find that some of your symptoms fall into more than one category. This is because anxiety affects people in different ways.

Following is a list of many of the most common symptoms experienced by those with anxiety disorders.

Panic Disorder

- numbness or tingling
- feeling hot
- wobbliness in legs
- inability to relax
- fear of the worst happening
- dizziness or lightheadedness
- pounding or racing heart
- unsteadiness
- feelings of terror
- nervousness
- feelings of choking
- trembling hands
- shakiness
- fear of losing control
- difficulty breathing
- fear of dying

- indigestion or nausea
- feeling faint
- flushed face
- cold sweat

Generalized Anxiety Disorder (GAD)

- worrying much of the time
- muscle tension
- restlessness, feeling keyed up
- irritability
- difficulty concentrating
- mind going blank
- easily fatigued

Phobia

- intense fear cued by the presence or anticipation

of a specific object or situation (for example, heights, enclosed spaces, or flying)
- marked feelings of anxiety when encountering that object or situation
- extreme avoidance of that object or situation

Social Phobia

- fear of failure
- fear of rejection
- fear of social ridicule
- intense fear of talking to strangers
- stage fright

CAUSES OF ANXIETY DISORDERS

There are actually many causes of excessive anxiety. And what causes *your* anxiety may not be the same as what causes another person's anxiety, even if you both have the same type of anxiety disorder.

You can become vulnerable to developing anxiety disorders because of a variety of biological, psychological, and social factors. These factors make up your biopsychosocial experience. Biological factors include genetics and neurochemistry, such as a family history of anxiety disorders. Brain-based conditioning and psychological factors involve your early attachment relationship with your parents and the quality of your relationships with your family members. For example, if your parents made you feel anxious, rather than comforted, around them, you can be prone to anxiety. Psychological factors also include your cognitive skills. If you think in black-and-white terms or hold yourself to extreme perfectionist standards, you're likely to experience anxiety. Social factors include how well you adjust to your culture, ethnicity, and social situations, such as work, social gatherings, and cultural expectations. These factors comprise who you are and how you adapt to the world. None of them acts independently.

Each dimension of your biopsychosocial experience overlaps the others. The biological aspect involves your physical sensations, such as when you experience a rapid heartbeat or sweating. If you misinterpret these physical sensations as cause for alarm, you tend to increase your anxiety and might even experience a panic attack, leading you to believe that you are having a heart attack. The result is that you become extremely fearful of those physical sensations, doing everything you can to avoid them in the future. Or perhaps your palms sweat and your voice quivers a little when you meet new people. Becoming extremely concerned that someone might notice stirs up more anxiety, which contributes to an increase in sweaty palms and your voice quivering.

The psychological part of your biopsychosocial experience involves what you say to yourself when you experience anxiety. If you are a pessimist, a black-and-white thinker, or tend to catastrophize if things don't go perfectly, you'll stir up more anxiety. For example, say you encounter an unanticipated snag in your effort to complete a project. You could be flexible and roll with the bumps on the road, or you could say to yourself, "Everything's falling apart! Now what am I going to do?" Your pessimism and inflexibility set you up to see a bump as more than a bump—it's an impassable boulder in the road, a catastrophe.

Your "mood state" also affects how you think about and interpret the events in your life. When you're in particular mood, your thoughts can be colored by that mood. You make statements to yourself about what you are experiencing at any given moment, and if those statements are colored by an anxious state of mind, they can perpetuate anxiety.

The social aspect of the biopsychosocial experience involves a fear that other people will see that you have an anxiety disorder, which can affect your relationship with them. If you are with people you don't know, for example, you might say to yourself, "What if he can tell that I'm nervous? He'll think I'm an idiot." Statements like these heighten your anxiety.

It's important to understand that you can heal your anxiety without knowing what caused it. You don't need to discover the initial cause of the anxiety before you can take steps to dissolve it.

Joanne's Fear of Dogs

Joanne came to see me because she had developed a phobia about dogs and wanted to find out what had caused it. She wondered whether dogs held some sort of symbolic significance. Perhaps she had experienced some kind of trauma while petting a dog or even a nightmare about dogs that she could not remember. She felt certain that if only she could find the key to unlock her fear, she could regain her freedom.

Joanne needed to deal with her phobia, because most of her neighbors owned dogs. That's when she came to see me. She wanted me to hypnotize her, so that I "could dig into the deep recesses of (her) mind to discover what went wrong."

I pointed out that the initial cause of her anxiety about dogs was far less important than what she increasingly did to compensate for it. And what she increasingly did was avoid walking in the neighborhood. Like the famous chaos theory analogy about a butterfly flapping its wings in the Maldives and creating a typhoon in the Indian Ocean, one day Joanne had had to walk on the other side of the street to avoid a large, aggressive dog running loose in the neighbor's yard. Although the dog frightened her, she didn't find the experience traumatizing at the time. However, she began to feel anxious when she walked in the neighborhood and started to avoid walking outside, taking the car instead. Over time, she stopped going outside altogether.

Joanne didn't need to know what had sparked her phobia; it was more important that she focus on changing the way she was dealing with her anxiety about dogs. She needed to stop avoiding her fear and return to walking on her neighborhood sidewalks.

Medical Problems That Contribute to Anxiety

If you suffer from a major health problem, some of the symptoms of your condition can resemble the symptoms of anxiety. Being unaware of the origins of these symptoms can cause you to believe that you suffer from an anxiety disorder. The symptoms of mitral valve prolapse (see below), for example, are similar to those experienced during a panic attack. Overreacting to these physical sensations without understanding their origin can actually spur on a real panic attack. If you have a medical condition that is associated with anxiety symptoms, seek treatment.

Following are some common conditions that can cause anxiety-like symptoms.

Mitral Valve Prolapse (MVP) A heart disorder that occurs when the valve between your heart's left upper chamber (left atrium) and your left lower chamber (left ventricle) doesn't close properly, MVP occurs in 2 percent of the general population. Approximately 50 percent of people with MVP experience chest pains, breathlessness, and palpitation, the same symptoms of a panic attack.

Exposure to Toxins The metabolic and toxic effects of either consuming or being exposed to chemicals and environmental toxins, such as hydrocarbons, mercury, and carbon dioxide, can cause or worsen anxiety symptoms. For example, many pesticides containing DDT, chlordane, lindane, and dieldrin can cause nervousness, insomnia, and nausea. Usually, the anxiety-like symptoms of exposure from the toxic chemicals fade once you get away from them. However, if you experienced major exposure to toxins, the severity of impairment will be greater.

Common Causes of Anxiety

- Genetics: inheriting an anxious or shy temperament
- Growing up with anxious parents who model their anxiety and worry about everything
- Poor attachment relationships with your parents or caregivers, making it hard for you to feel connected and comforted by other people
- Being criticized consistently while growing up, causing you to be overcritical of yourself
- Experiencing physical, sexual, or emotional abuse, which can cause you to feel undeserving of the good things in life
- Traumatic experiences that have a lingering effect by making you hypervigilant for similar trauma
- Side effects of medical problems and medications (see the following section)
- Embracing thinking styles, such as perfectionism and black-and-white thinking, that decrease your flexibility and adaptability
- Creating a biochemistry that stirs anxiety through poor eating habits
- Trying to avoid feeling any kind of stress

Medication Side Effects The side effects of many medications—monoamine oxidase inhibitors, calcium channel blockers, and theophylline, for example—can cause anxiety-like symptoms, which your primary care physician might not have warned you about. Over-the-counter medications, such as antihistamines, can also mimic anxiety symptoms. Talk to the pharmacist when you pick up your medication. Pharmacists usually know the side effects of various medications. Always read the medication information sheet that comes with the bottle.

Following is a list of other medical, health, and drug-related conditions that can produce anxiety-like symptoms:

- Endocrinological: hyperthyroidism, hypoglycemia, Cushing's syndrome, menopause, premenstrual syndrome, and pheochromocytoma
- Neurological: complex partial seizures, vestibular dysfunctions, head injuries
- Pulmonary: asthma, hyperventilation
- Cardiological: high blood pressure, chronic obstructive pulmonary disease (COPD), lung cancer
- Alcohol and benzodiazepine withdrawal
- Use of cocaine and marijuana
- Excessive caffeine consumption
- Deficiencies in magnesium, vitamin B_{12}, potassium, and calcium

If you have any of these medical conditions, work with your doctor to get comprehensive treatment. If you still suffer from anxiety, then the rest of this book can be helpful.

ASSESSING YOUR ANXIETY

To determine to what degree you're troubled by anxiety, it will be helpful to identify your symptoms. You will be referring back to this list when you perform some of the exercises in this book. From the following list, check off the symptoms that apply to you.

- numbness or tingling
- feeling hot
- wobbliness in legs
- inability to relax
- fear of the worst happening
- dizziness or lightheadedness
- pounding or racing heart
- unsteadiness
- feeling terrified

- nervousness
- feelings of choking
- trembling hands
- shakiness
- fear of losing control
- difficulty breathing
- fear of dying
- indigestion or nausea
- feeling faint
- flushed face
- cold sweat

- worrying much of the time
- muscle tension
- restlessness, feeling keyed up
- irritability
- difficulty concentrating
- mind going blank
- easily fatigued
- fear of failure
- fear of rejection
- fear of social ridicule

The more symptoms you checked off, the greater the role anxiety plays in your life. The list above is not exhaustive. You might experience symptoms that are not on the list. Write them down in the space below.

_____   _____
_____   _____
_____   _____
_____   _____
_____   _____
_____   _____
_____   _____
_____   _____
_____   _____
_____   _____

Assess the Severity of Your Symptoms

The next question to ask yourself is whether your symptoms have been increasing in severity. In general, the more severe your anxiety symptoms, the more they negatively impact your life. However, the severity of the symptoms also increases over time. This alarming tendency occurs if you make efforts to *avoid* the situations that make you anxious. Not surprisingly, the higher the severity of your symptoms, the greater the potential for avoidance. If your anxiety is severe, it can start to impinge on your life. Take a look at what happened to Cynthia.

Cynthia Shrinks Her World

Cynthia, a graduate student in history, came to my anxiety class because she feared driving on the freeway. Whenever she was in a car on the freeway, she started to panic, so she started to avoid them. Sometimes she added hours to her commute to avoid the freeways. Soon, she was feeling anxious about driving in general. Even driving on the city streets made her anxious.

Cynthia decided that she would retreat to her comfort level, so that she could regroup to gather her strength. Once she "felt ready again," she would drive again, not only on the city streets but also on the freeways.

As time went on, however, Cynthia grew to feel *more*, not less, anxious about driving. She felt like she was falling into quicksand, sinking day by day into feeling anxious all the time. One day, she told her husband, who was becoming frustrated because he had become her taxi service, that she felt she was "having a mental breakdown."

Cynthia's anxiety about driving on the freeways was interfering with her life. In the space below, write down the sensations that interfere with your life and keep you from doing the things you want and need to do. By identifying these sensations, you will be in a better position to confront and neutralize them in the exercises that follow. The end result will be that they won't stand in the way of you enjoying your life.

WHAT SENSATIONS INTERFERE WITH YOUR LIFE?

_____   _____

_____   _____

_____   _____

_____   _____

_____   _____

_____   _____

_____   _____

_____   _____

_____   _____

_____   _____

_____   _____

_____   _____

_____   _____

_____   _____

_____   _____

_____   _____

The following chart is a measure of severity. It is called the Subjective Units of Distress Scale, or SUDS for short. The SUDS method of measuring the severity of anxiety will help you target the anxiety situations that need to be addressed and to gauge your progress. You'll be referring to this chart throughout the rest of the workbook.

SUBJECTIVE UNITS OF DISTRESS SCALE (SUDS)

RATING	SEVERITY	DESCRIPTION
0	none	You feel no distress or anxiety. You are absolutely calm and relaxed.
10	minimal	You feel mostly calm, but have a twinge of tension or alertness that isn't very noticeable.
20	mild	You feel slightly tense or nervous, but are still able to focus on your work or social activities.
30	mild	You feel mildly stressed, tense, or nervous. You can work or socialize, but you have to actively manage the anxiety in some way, and you might be irritable. Your body may be tense or "keyed up."
40	moderate	You feel mild-to-moderate anxiety, and are somewhat distracted or irritable. You have mild physical symptoms, such as muscle tension, shakiness, or feeling weak.
50	moderate	You are moderately anxious or stressed, and it is interfering somewhat with your ability to focus or work. You are distracted, hyperalert, and on your guard. Physical symptoms can include increased heart rate, lightheadedness, butterflies, and irregular breathing.
60	moderate	You are very anxious, distracted, and hypervigilant. You might feel dizzy, lightheaded, or shaky, with rapid heart rate, tightness in the chest, and nausea.
70	severe	You are intensely anxious or stressed, with strong physical symptoms. You are having difficulty concentrating on anything but the anxiety.
80	severe	Your anxiety is very intense and overwhelming, with significant physical symptoms (pounding heart, rapid breathing, sweating, dizziness, nausea). You are focused on wanting to get out of the situation.
90	extreme	You are in a state of extreme fear and distress and are having difficulty coping. Physical sensations are intense, and you are entirely focused on escaping the situation.
100	extreme	You are in full panic mode and fear you may die, faint, or lose your mind. Your fear is so intense that you are overwhelmed and can only think of escape.

Paula's Increasing Anxiety

Paula came to my anxiety class after experiencing increasing anxiety for two months. She described the following symptoms: shortness of breath, sweating, trembling, rapid heartbeat, dizziness, and chest pain. These periodic and overwhelming physical sensations came in bursts lasting about ten minutes. When she experienced these "attacks," she couldn't think of anything else. She said, "It felt like my world was falling apart!"

For the next exercise, use the SUDS chart to determine the degree of anxiety that you are experiencing. Apply a SUDS score to each symptom in the blank worksheet below. To give you an example, I have shown how Paula filled out her SUDS worksheet.

PAULA'S SUDS SCORES

SYMPTOMS	SUDS
shortness of breath	90
rapid heartbeat	87
sweating	80
trembling	71
dizziness	68
chest pain	55

Based on her responses, Paula was suffering from a fear of her physical sensations. She described how they came out of the blue and overwhelmed her. This symptom constellation indicates that Paula was suffering from panic disorder.

In the chart below, write your symptoms and their SUDS, starting with the most severe.

SYMPTOM SEVERITY WORKSHEET

SYMPTOMS	SUDS

You will be referring back to these exercises throughout the later chapters of the book. The information about your symptoms and your SUDS will be useful to give you an idea of whether you *are* suffering from an anxiety disorder and, if so, what type of disorder you have. In the next chapter, you'll learn about the various types of anxiety disorders. You'll be able to diagnose yourself and learn how to treat your particular anxiety through the exercises in the rest of the book.

Chapter 2
Types of Anxiety Disorders

Anxiety is a general term to describe a state of worry, uneasiness, or apprehension. As you learned in chapter 1, everyone has some anxiety. That's normal. However, when anxiety becomes overwhelming and debilitating, it becomes an anxiety disorder. There are different types of anxiety disorders. They include panic disorder, phobias, general anxiety disorder, obsessive-compulsive disorder, and post-traumatic stress disorder. In this chapter, you'll learn to identify the types of anxiety and determine whether you suffer from them.

Some of what you will be learning in the coming chapters addresses a particular type of anxiety. The thing to remember about these types is that there is considerable overlap. This is because there are many common symptoms among the main types of anxiety disorders. What distinguishes them are such factors as duration and timing (constant versus episodic). The symptoms of panic disorder, for example, are periodic and intense; the symptoms of general anxiety disorder (GAD) are constant and less intense.

The situations that trigger the symptoms and the severity of your anxiety differ from person to person. A phobia, for example, may result in anxiety only when encountering that object (spiders, for example) or situation (driving on freeways).

The major types of anxiety disorders—the ones you'll learn about in this chapter—are panic disorder (PD), generalized anxiety disorder (GAD), and phobias. I'll also briefly discuss adjustment disorder with anxiety. Two other major anxiety disorders, obsessive-compulsive disorder (OCD) and post-traumatic stress disorder (PTSD), will not be covered in this book. Although some of the methods you'll learn can be applied to those disorders, this book will focus on ways to overcome the ones I list below.

If you feel that you have a little of one disorder and a little of another, you aren't alone. Your anxiety can include a combination of disorders. For example, you might have GAD and experience periodic panic attacks or have a phobia and experience panic attacks when you encounter that feared object or situation. Combinations occur because many of the same brain systems are operating together. (See chapter 3 for more on the brain and how it works.)

DETERMINING YOUR ANXIETY TYPE

People who suffer from anxiety often experience distress in the form of symptom *clusters*. These clusters indicate a particular type of anxiety disorder. For example, a cluster of symptoms that include rapid heartbeat, shortness of breath, and sweating occurring together represents panic disorder. A cluster that includes tension, general nervousness, insomnia, and excessive worrying represents GAD.

Ted's Symptom Cluster
Ted, a thirty-seven-year-old insurance underwriter, identified the following symptom cluster.

I worry all the time.
I feel tense, and my shoulders ache.
I can't get to sleep at night because my mind is going a hundred miles an hour.
I expect the worst, always wondering when the other shoe is going to drop.

Ted's symptoms cluster around what is called *free-floating anxiety,* a state of being anxious most of the time. He complained that he just couldn't relax. "I feel tense all the time, like something terrible is going to happen." The severity of his anxiety wasn't extreme, but it was like chronic pain, always there, wearing him down. Ted was suffering from GAD.

What symptom clusters can you identify for yourself? Write them down below. You'll be coming back to this list later, to determine your type of anxiety disorder.

WHAT ARE YOUR SYMPTOM CLUSTERS?

_____   _____
_____   _____
_____   _____
_____   _____
_____   _____
_____   _____
_____   _____
_____   _____
_____   _____
_____   _____
_____   _____
_____   _____

Panic Disorder

Panic disorder (PD) is the most dramatic and frightening type of anxiety disorder, because it involves *panic attacks.* If you have PD, you tend to experience bursts of seemingly uncontrollable physical and psychological symptoms that usually occur out of the blue, making you feel intense fear. Your physical symptoms can include a racing heart, shortness of breath, and chest pain; your psychological symptoms can include a fear of dying or going crazy. These are symptoms of a panic attack. During a panic attack, you feel an overwhelming rush of anxiety. This surge of anxiety is periodic. You never know when it's going to happen next. Panic attacks are referred to as "attacks," because that's what they feel like. They seem to *just happen,* that you have no control over them.

These physical sensations don't cause panic attacks. What causes them is your *reaction* to the physical sensations. Say that you are experiencing a major period of stress at work, with a deadline you can't meet. As you spin your wheels trying to meet the deadline, the reality that you can't meet it causes an overwhelming feeling of stress, along with symptoms in the form of shortness of breath, rapid heartbeat, sweating, headaches, and nausea. You can react to these symptoms in two ways: You can see them for what they are—a physical reaction to stress—or you can consider them an alarm for something more ominous, such as a heart attack. When you overreact to those symptoms, you can tumble into a panic attack.

Panic attacks are triggered by a false alarm: your belief that the sensations you are experiencing are signs of some greater problem. If you react to them as if they were a real alarm, you trigger the *fight-or-flight response,* which is why, during a panic attack, you feel an intense need to flee from something terrible. The problem is that you don't know what that terrible thing might be. Some people feel the need to get to an emergency room, because they fear they are having a heart attack.

What is the fight-or-flight response? It's a physiological response to a threat. We inherited it from our ancestors, who were often confronted with life-threatening situations. When one of those ancestors faced a predator, for example, his body began to undergo physiological changes to prepare itself to fight or take flight. His body pumped adrenaline to make his heart beat rapidly, causing blood to flow to his extremities to ready them for action. His breathing became rapid and shallow, to charge up his body and quickly oxygenate his blood. He perspired to cool his overheated body, and his muscles tensed, to brace for quick movements at any time. Finally, his attention narrowed to focus solely on the danger and prevent distraction.

We still have this fight-or-flight mechanism. The problem for people who suffer from panic disorder is that these physical sensations get triggered when there is *no reason* to fight or flee. They're triggered by false alarms.

These false alarms can arise for a number of reasons. You might have developed a habit of thinking or feeling that danger exists where it does not. Or you have a tendency to misread physical symptoms, such as dry mouth, nausea, and dizziness, as cause for alarm and overreact to them. Perhaps you are a pessimist, and, when things don't go right, you panic.

During a panic attack, the physical sensations can occur out of the blue. When you overreact to them with fearful thoughts ("I can't breathe!"), you trigger more physical sensations, which fuel *more* fearful thoughts ("I'm having a heart attack!"). This chain of events is associated with a wide range of physical and psychological symptoms.

Panic Disorder Assessment Test

Check the symptoms that apply to you:

Physical Symptoms

- shortness of breath
- rapid heartbeat
- lightheadedness
- chest pain
- sweating
- dizziness
- numbness or tingling
- nausea

Psychological Symptoms

- mind going blank
- difficulty concentrating
- fear that you're going crazy
- fear that you're going to die
- racing thoughts
- feelings of doom
- fear that you're losing control

If you checked a few symptoms from the physical column and a few from the psychological column, it's possible that you have a panic disorder. What you do and what you think when you experience these symptoms can contribute to the development of a panic disorder. Next, answer these questions by circling Yes or No.

- Have you ever gone to the emergency room when experiencing the symptoms listed above because you thought you were having a heart attack? **Yes / No**
- Have you come to expect a burst of panic symptoms to appear out of the blue? **Yes / No**
- Despite the fact that these episodes lasted less than ten minutes, did you think they would last forever? **Yes / No**
- Are you so ashamed of these attacks that you do things to hide the symptoms? **Yes / No**
- Do you avoid situations to keep from having attacks? **Yes / No**
- Does your life center around whether or not you have these attacks? **Yes / No**
- Are you so overwhelmed with physical sensations, such as shortness of breath, rapid heartbeat, hot flashes, dizziness, and chest pain, that you have asked your doctor for medication for each one? **Yes / No**
- Do you believe these episodes are completely out of your control? **Yes / No**
- If these episodes have increased over time, do you think that it is a sign that the situation is hopeless? **Yes / No**

If you answered yes to any of the previous questions, your actions are actually contributing to the panic attacks. You are stirring up more anxiety than is healthy.

Ian Learns to Avoid Overreacting to Panic Sensations

Ian began to suffer from periodic panic attacks while in his late twenties, when he took a job that he felt he was not prepared to handle. When he was at work, or just thought about going to work, his heart would begin to beat rapidly, he hyperventilated, his hands would sweat, and eventually his chest would hurt. Within a very short period of time, his thoughts would race and he would become lightheaded.

Although he quit that job and went on to one he was more suited to, Ian continued having panic attacks. Because he was no longer at the job that caused him so much stress, Ian assumed that the symptoms he was experiencing must be a sign of a serious health problem, a series of heart attacks, perhaps. After twice going to the emergency room, he was referred to me.

Initially, Ian remained convinced that he had a heart problem. He said he had no control over his symptoms, that they happened out of the blue and seemed to take over. Eventually, I helped him understand that he had developed a panic disorder.

During anxiety class, Ian learned that he had a tendency to panic about his physical sensations of anxiety. He came to understand that his plight had much to do with the well-known quote, "There's nothing to fear but fear itself." Fear seemed to be driving his panic. Once Ian understood that he was having panic attacks, not heart attacks, he began to develop the skills he needed to control the symptoms.

Instead of overreacting to his physical sensations, Ian learned to shift to an observing and accepting attitude.

Panic Disorder and Depression

Panic disorder can occur with other anxiety disorders. As many as 50 percent of people with panic disorder have GAD, phobias, and OCD, as well as disorders such as depression. If you have PD and also suffer from depression, note that depression can complicate your efforts to overcome panic disorder. You can be less motivated do the work necessary to try new skills, and when you do accomplish anything, you tend to negatively appraise it. Also, because depression generally lowers your physiological arousal, you might not make adequate use of interoceptive exposure. For these reasons, you should get help with your depression before or simultaneously with learning how to heal your anxiety.

He began to understand that his physical sensations were just sensations. They weren't cause for alarm, nor were they symptoms of a heart attack. Ian learned to experience the physical sensations without overreacting to them and to simply "ride them out." He learned to override his overreactions. By using this interoceptive exposure technique (which you'll learn more about in chapter 9), Ian found that each time he experienced the sensations associated with the early signs of a panic attack, their severity lessened. Soon, he learned to defuse panic attacks before they occurred.

Ian also learned to replace his negative self-talk with positive self-talk. For example, instead of saying to himself, "Something terrible is going to happen," he said, "I've been through this many times before and got through it fine. It gets easier each time, if I keep this in mind."

GENERALIZED ANXIETY DISORDER (GAD)

If you suffer from GAD, you tend to worry excessively about your future, health, family, friends, and safety. You also probably feel tense and anxious much of the time. You might think of yourself as a chronic worrier and can torture yourself with "what-if" thoughts throughout the day: "What if the house door isn't locked?" or "What if the boss throws another project at me?" or "What if the car breaks down on the way to the airport?" The constant anxiety causes you to overreact to stress, and you create more anxiety.

GAD differs from panic disorder and phobias in that the anxiety is like chronic pain. Although the free-floating anxiety and worry are not intense, they seem to be there all the time. The symptoms of GAD can intensify from time to time, depending on the situation. For example, though your anxiety level might be a constant background hum throughout the day, when your boss walks into the room, your anxiety can peak, and you can experience a panic attack.

GAD Assessment Test

Check the symptoms you experience on a constant basis.

- muscle tension
- restlessness
- feeling on edge
- mind going blank
- easily fatigued
- problems sleeping

- constant worry
- dry mouth
- clammy hands
- feeling shaky
- trembling

If you checked four of these symptoms, and experience these symptoms for more days than not for at least six months, you probably suffer from GAD.

Sara Learns to Manage Her GAD

Prior to coming to the class, Sara had for many years been plagued by constant worry and unceasing tension. It was hard for her to sleep at night because she couldn't turn off her mind. During the day, she felt exhausted and tense at the same time. One day, she felt so nervous that she rushed out of a staff meeting.

Sara's symptoms suggested that she was suffering from GAD. She talked a mile a minute and didn't seem to take time to breathe between sentences. As she talked, she seemed to ramp up her anxiety. She admitted skipping meals and drinking coffee instead. She rarely got any exercise and felt tired all the time.

We started Sara's recovery by changing her breathing pattern. I asked her to pause between sentences and breathe. As we went through breathing exercises, I noticed that she became much calmer. With encouragement, she began to practice breathing and talking more slowly on a regular basis.

Sara also had to change her diet. She started eating regular balanced meals and cut back on the caffeine. Although her shift in breathing and the change in diet contributed some relief in anxiety, Sara did continue to experience a low level of background anxiety. This was a big improvement over her previous anxiety level, but there was still much to accomplish.

We next turned to how Sara tormented herself with negative self-talk. Whatever the situation, Sara managed to turn it into a negative. Her negative self-talk caused her to think of everything that happened as anxious and depressing experiences. Because she expected negatives and viewed everything as overwhelming, that's what her experience came to be. We worked on transforming these negative thought patterns into reasonable assessments of any given situation. She neutralized the negative self-talk and became more open to positive experiences. She soon began to feel like a "new person."

Finally, we turned to her poor sleep pattern. We employed a number of sleep hygiene techniques (more on these in chapter 5), and her sleep gradually improved. Through a combination of breathing work, change in diet, a shift away from negative self-talk, and sleep hygiene techniques, Sara found that she was calmer and more focused during the day.

PHOBIAS

If you have a phobia, your anxiety is connected to a specific type of stress trigger. You experience an intense fear of specific objects, situations, or environments. For example, the most common phobia is fear of public speaking. Other phobias include fear of flying, meeting new people, crossing bridges, driving, being in large crowds, heights, and enclosures.

Types of Phobias

There are many types of phobia. Here are some common ones:

- **Acrophobia:** fear of heights
- **Claustrophobia:** fear of enclosed spaces
- **Agoraphobia:** fear of the outside
- **Arachnophobia:** fear of spiders
- **Social phobia:** fear of social situations
- **Doctor or dentist phobia:** fear of seeing doctors or dentists
- **Animal phobia:** fear of certain animals, such as snakes or bears

- **Airplane phobia:** fear of flying on airplanes
- **Thunder or lightening phobia:** fear of large thunderstorms
- **Bridge phobia:** fear of crossing bridges
- **Elevator phobia:** fear of using an elevator

Some not-so-common phobias involve a fear of:

- blood
- water
- darkness
- injections
- illness
- insects
- driving on freeways

- going to the store
- eating in restaurants
- going to work
- being alone
- going into tunnels
- going into a public restroom

Do you intensely fear any of the objects or situations listed above? Note that simply feeling more anxious about driving on the freeway than on city streets doesn't necessarily indicate a phobia. But if your fear of driving on the freeway is so great that you avoid it altogether and drive for an extra hour on side streets, you have a phobia.

Do you have fears that are not listed on the previous page? List them below. Remember that these are fears that alter the way you live. Taking a bus across the country, instead of taking an airplane, because you fear flying constitutes a phobia. This list will be useful to refer back to when you practice some of the exercises in chapter 8.

PHOBIA SELF-ASSESSMENT TEST

_____   _____

_____   _____

_____   _____

_____   _____

_____   _____

_____   _____

_____   _____

_____   _____

Sonya's Expanding Supermarket Phobia

Sonya came to see me because she developed a phobia about going to supermarkets. Her fear was so great that she was forced to ask her friends and family to pick up groceries for her. By the time she came to see me, she was in the process of destroying those friendships and straining family ties. Sonya felt that her problem was getting worse. She worried that there would come a time when she wouldn't be able to go to other stores, either. As she predicted, in time, even the thought of going into a store made Sonya feel a surge of anxiety, and she quit shopping altogether. When her husband insisted she get help, she came to see me.

I explained that her tendency to avoid going into grocery stores and then into any store had created an overwhelming wall of anxiety. She needed to avoid her avoidant behaviors. She thought I was joking, at first, because the idea sounded ridiculous to her. "Why not avoid things that bother me?" she asked. I explained that avoiding her fears only made her anxiety worse.

Social Phobia

If you experience anxiety in situations such as meeting new people or being in a room with strangers and go out of your way to avoid these situations, you likely suffer from a social phobia.

Social phobia has a number of variants, including fear of:

- public speaking
- dating
- parties or social occasions
- meeting new people
- crowds
- taking exams

- writing or signing documents in the presence of others
- choking or spilling food while eating in public
- blushing
- talking in class

Remember that experiencing a little fear in social situations is common. Many people fear public speaking. It's the degree of fear that sets anxiety apart from social phobia. Ask yourself whether you are debilitated by the fear. Perhaps you have an extreme fear of talking to strangers. That is a social phobia.

What social situations do you fear? Write them in the space below. This list will help you target specific phobic social structures to defuse as you go through the exercises in this workbook.

IDENTIFY YOUR SOCIAL FEARS

_____   _____

_____   _____

_____   _____

_____   _____

_____   _____

_____   _____

_____   _____

_____   _____

_____   _____

_____   _____

Social Anxiety Disorder (SAD)

Social anxiety disorder (SAD) is a type of social anxiety. If you have SAD, you have a marked and persistent fear of particular social situations that expose you to unfamiliar people or to possible scrutiny by others. You fear that you will show anxiety symptoms or act in a way that will be humiliating or embarrassing.

When you are exposed to certain social situations, you tend to be overwhelmed with anxiety and might even experience a panic attack. Like others with social phobia, your response is to avoid social situations, and, when you can't, you endure these situations with intense anxiety or distress.

SAD can take many forms and can impair you in different degrees. Some people feel anxious around authority figures, such as police officers, teachers, or employers. Some are anxious when there are more than three people in the room, some when they're around anyone they don't know. Some fear that they are being observed by others. They fear being seen blushing, eating, or doing something that might be regarded negatively—they fear being scrutinized for being anxious.

Just like others who experience a phobia, SAD sufferers tend to avoid the situations that make them anxious. In time, they can discover that their fears have grown and their world has shrunk. Overcoming social anxiety disorder involves the same reconditioning and exposure techniques used to defeat any phobia.

The more you avoid social situations, the greater your phobia becomes. This is because you afford yourself little opportunity to habituate to social situations. If you avoid social situations, the fear will grow. This fact, in some ways, is counterintuitive because you feel "better" immediately after avoiding what you fear.

Social Phobia Assessment Test

For the most part, do you:

- do whatever you can to avoid talking to people?

- turn down social invitations?

- leave, if more than three people enter the room?

- avoid thinking of social situations?

If you checked one or more of boxes, you might have a social phobia.

To overcome social phobia, you need to practice exercises to "recondition" yourself, by gradually increasing your social exposure. These exposure exercises work for other types of phobias, as well. In chapter 8, you'll learn how to stop *avoiding* what you fear and instead *expose* yourself to what you fear. With repeated exposure, you'll eventually lose your fear and become more comfortable in social situations. As you see yourself function in the social arena by practicing social skills, you will be less likely to have a phobic reaction.

Tonya's Struggle with Social Phobia

Tonya was referred to me by her primary care physician, who was concerned about her intense anxiety during a physical exam. After considerable effort to build rapport, he finally convinced her to come in and see me.

She told me that she felt extremely nervous around anyone who wasn't family. Despite being twenty-three years old, Tonya had only two friends, whom she had known since elementary school. She had dropped out of college several times because she couldn't get herself to go to class. She told me that she always had been painfully shy and the prospect of having to meet people or talk in class made her panic. She said, "I kept signing up, figuring that I would go when I felt comfortable. But I never did. Just the thought of being with all those strangers was too much to take."

I asked her come to my anxiety class. Predictably, she balked. She did, however, agree to another appointment. It took two more sessions to talk her into coming to the class. I agreed that she would not be pressured to speak in class but that I wanted her to work on it.

I told the class that we were to practice talking. Nobody in the class knew anyone else. Although I told Tonya that she could sit the first exercise out, she decided to try and participate because the potential social anxiety of sitting on the sidelines was greater than what she would incur by making an effort. I asked everyone to introduce themselves to the person sitting next to them, then took them through a series of questions to ask each other. After a while, they started to laugh because of the stilted quality of the questions. The humor loosened them up, Tonya included, and they began to ask more spontaneous questions of one another. A little later, I reminded them that they had all done what they feared, namely meet new people and break into spontaneous conversation. The next step was to move outside their comfort zone and meet new people outside of class.

Tonya was ambivalent about agreeing to any exercises outside of class. Meanwhile, her peers were taking on the exposure tasks and successfully meeting the challenges. Tonya decided to take the first step: striking up a conversation with our receptionist, who she saw each time she registered for the class but to whom she had not actually spoken a word.

With the support of her peers in the class, and despite some reticence, she succeeded in striking up a conversation. Eventually, Tonya came in early each class to talk to the receptionist. The success of that experience opened the door for her to consider other social exposures and "practice sessions," as she learned to call them.

Over the next several weeks, Tonya applied for and attended two college classes. Although she was initially overwhelmed by the anticipatory anxiety, she managed to stick to her plan of "practice sessions." Tonya never became the life of the party, but she got over her paralyzing fear of meeting people and, in time, began to enjoy meeting people.

Adjustment Disorder with Anxiety

If you have recently experienced a great deal of stress associated with a major life event, such as divorce, taking on a challenging new job, or moving, you may experience a surge of anxiety with symptoms similar to GAD; you might even have a few panic attacks. This is a reaction to an out-of-the-ordinary stressor. Often the anxiety goes away when the stressor goes away. If the anxiety persists after the stressor goes away, it can develop into one of the anxiety disorders described above. This occurs if, during the anxiety phase of an adjustment, you avoid situations or experiences that make you anxious and then continue with the avoidance.

Using the exercises and techniques in this book can help alleviate your anxiety, even if it doesn't develop into a major disorder. They can also help you cope with your stressors until they pass.

In the next chapter, I'll introduce you to your brain. By knowing it better, you'll be able to use it more effectively, so that you can neutralize anxiety.

Chapter 3
Rewiring Your Brain

Learning how your brain and body work can give you a tangible understanding of your anxiety disorder and a sense of hope that you can gain mastery over it. In this chapter, you'll discover how your brain works and how understanding its functions can help reduce your anxiety.

You'll learn which parts of your brain are overactive and which are underactive when you're anxious and how you can use your brain to experience less anxiety. Think of this chapter and the one that follows as a tune-up manual for your brain.

GETTING TO KNOW YOUR BRAIN

Although your brain weighs only three pounds, it contains 100 billion nerve cells, called *neurons,* and many more support cells. More powerful than any computer, your brain is not hardwired—it can create or reduce anxiety, according to what you do and how you think. Discovering how your brain works can help you use it to reduce your anxiety.

Let's start with the big picture: your brain's architecture.

The Left and Right Hemispheres

Your brain has a right and a left hemisphere, each with unique talents and emotional tendencies. Your *right* hemisphere is talented at getting the "big picture," or gist, of a situation. It is generally more creative and activates when you learn something new. Once you learn a skill, it often is encoded in your *left* hemisphere, where routines, linear sequencing, and language are processed. Your right hemisphere processes negative emotions, and your left hemisphere processes positive emotions.

The Cerebral Cortex

The outer surface of your two hemispheres is called the *cortex,* which means "bark." When you look at a picture of the brain, you're seeing mostly cortex. The cortex is actually very thin, only 1.5 to 3 millimeters thick. It's in this part, the "gray matter," that most of your thinking takes place. Below the cortex is "white matter," which consists of support cells covering the long nerve fibers that connect various parts of your brain.

Each of your two hemispheres has four major parts, called lobes. In each set of lobes are primary areas that are specialized for certain skills. For example, your occipital lobes specialize in vision; your temporal lobes in hearing, memory, and recognition; the parietal lobes in sensing physical sensation; and your frontal lobes in movement, problem-solving, and initiating behaviors.

Adjacent to the primary lobe areas are association areas, where input from other areas of the brain is processed. For example, the part of your left temporal lobe called Wernicke's Area helps you make sense of what is being said to you. In your left frontal lobe, located in front of the primary area that controls movement, is an association area called Broca's Area, which helps you speak.

Your Peripheral Nervous System

Your peripheral nervous system, which controls your body, is divided into two parts: the voluntary (also called the somatic) and the involuntary (also called the autonomic). Your somatic nervous system is voluntary: it operates when you decide to move a limb or stand up. Your autonomic nervous system operates automatically. It maintains homeostasis; it makes sure that your body systems operate in balance. Your autonomic nervous system can get activated, or it can calm down. It can turn off the fight-or-flight mode when you don't need it on.

Your autonomic nervous system also has two branches: the *sympathetic* nervous system, which regulates arousal, and the *parasympathetic* nervous system, which regulates relaxation. Your sympathetic branch activates your brain and body with neurotransmitters such as norepinephrine and epinephrine (adrenaline). The parasympathetic branch helps you calm down by releasing the brain neurotransmitter GABA, which acts to dampen the effects of adrenaline and to calm down your amygdala. You can learn how to turn on your parasympathetic system.

The Amygdala and Hippocampus

Deep within your temporal lobes are two structures that are involved in memory and play different roles in anxiety. They are the *amygdala* and the *hippocampus*. The amygdala, from *amygdalon*, the Latin word for "almond," was named by early anatomists for its almond shape. It is the center of fear and tends to be hypersensitive in people with anxiety disorders. The hippocampus, named for its seahorse shape, helps you remember what is—and what is not—worthy of fear.

Your hippocampus and amygdala control two types of memory: *explicit* and *implicit*. You use your hippocampus in explicit memory when you try to remember what you had for dinner last night, when you have that appointment to go to the dentist, and what the name is of that familiar-looking woman standing in the checkout line at the grocery store. These are facts, dates, words, and events. It is this type of memory that people often complain they are losing.

Your amygdala controls a significant part of your implicit, or emotional, memory. It reacts unconsciously to events and situations that are potentially dangerous and activates the *fear circuit* in your body, known as the fight-or-flight response. Your amygdala triggers the fight-or-flight response via your hypothalamus-pituitary-adrenal axis (HPA).

Here's how the process works: At the first sign of danger, the amygdala signals your hypothalamus to secrete a substance called cortical-releasing factor, or CRF. CRF in turn alerts your pituitary gland to release another substance called ACTH into your bloodstream. ACTH triggers your adrenal glands to release epinephrine and norepinephrine, two types of the brain chemicals called *neurotransmitters*. They charge up your sympathetic nervous system. About thirty minutes later, if stress persists, a stress hormone called cortisol is released to keep you activated. Cortisol further excites your amygdala.

This activation system makes evolutionary sense, because if our ancestors encountered danger in specific situations, they would want to remember that emotionally. In other words, feeling anxiety when in a particular situation, such as being too close to a lion's den, reminds them that the den is dangerous. In the modern world, of course, most of us are not likely to regularly encounter a lion's den. Yet, the memory system still exists. And once it gets turned on, it's hard to turn it off.

This alarm system is automatic; that is, it happens before your cortex (the part of your brain that does the thinking) has time to think about it. When your prehistoric ancestors encountered a lion, it was best to react immediately and not stand around admiring its mane, or wondering why it's bothering you and not tracking down some tasty antelope. Your amygdala and the HPA axis kept your ancestors alive, so they could have children, which thousands of years later made you possible. You inherited the same rapid-response fight-or-flight system.

Your amygdala stirs enough fear in you to pull your car to the side of the road during a violent rainstorm or to react when you encounter a pit bull. This is normal and a good thing! However, if another car plows into you, or if the pit bull attacks, your amygdala can become oversensitive the next time you are in a rainstorm or encounter a pit bull. Having these experiences will *not* necessarily cause you to develop a panic disorder. But if you refuse to drive when it rains, or you stay away from all dogs, the fear of these encounters grows and *can* contribute to your developing an anxiety disorder. If you avoid rainstorms or dogs, your amygdala doesn't have an opportunity to adjust to the fact that rainstorms and dogs aren't necessarily dangerous. Consequently, you'll feel fear when you don't need to feel fear and anxiety.

Fortunately, you can tame your amygdala when it gets overactivated. You can do this by exposing yourself to rainstorms and dogs. By activating another part of your brain, such as your frontal lobes, while you are in rainstorms or petting a dog and telling yourself that there is nothing to fear, you can tame your amygdala and avoid developing a phobia of rainstorms or dogs. To rewire your brain to inhibit anxiety and strengthen the connections between your frontal lobes and amygdala, you'll need to expose yourself to dogs or rainstorms often.

Your Frontal Lobes

Of particular importance to anxiety are your frontal lobes. A sort of brain within the brain, your frontal lobes are sometimes called the "executive brain" because they orchestrate the resources of the rest of your brain. We have the largest frontal lobes of any species. For example, our frontal lobes comprise 20 percent of our brain; a cat's frontal lobes, by contrast, comprise only 3 percent of its brain. That alone says a lot about the difference between our species. Cats don't think about anxiety or read books about it. When they become anxious around someone, it's extraordinarily hard for them to learn *not* to be anxious around that person. Humans can make such changes more quickly. That's because our frontal lobes decide what to do, how to stay positive, and how to appreciate the larger picture of life.

Your frontal lobes are not the same. The left and right frontal lobes deal with emotions differently, just as your left and right hemispheres do. Your *left* frontal lobe is skillful at labeling emotion and putting a positive spin on your experiences. It promotes taking action. Your *right* frontal lobe is good at grasping the big picture. However, when your right frontal lobe becomes overactivated and is not balanced by the involvement of the left frontal lobe, you can feel overwhelmed and anxious. This is because your right frontal lobe promotes withdrawal and passive behaviors. To counterbalance the right frontal lobe, you need to take action. Taking action activates your left frontal lobe and its positive emotions; being passive activates your right frontal lobe and its negative (anxious) emotions.

Certain areas of your frontal lobes have different functions relevant to anxiety. The *orbital frontal cortex* (right behind the orbs of your eyes), for example, can be talented at controlling emotions, if it is "taught" to do this. It can shut down the fear network or, alternatively, hijack it—it exerts inhibitory control over your amygdala. The orbital frontal cortex learns how to control emotions, such as anxiety, from the way your parents taught you to control them, when you were growing up.

Along with the other parts of your brain that comprise what has been called the "social brain," your orbital frontal cortex thrives on social interaction. In fact, from the first few minutes of life, your bonding experiences with your parents helped develop this social brain. Your later relationships modified those neural connections. Social support can help this part of your brain organize its inhibitory control over our amygdala and the fear associated with it.

The socially sensitive parts of your brain can help you lessen your anxiety and tame your amygdala. Brain cells referred to as *mirror neurons* are acutely sensitive to the intentions of others. They allow you to mirror another person's emotions—to feel what they feel. They are essentially the brain-based explanation of empathy.

Positive relationships enhance your sense of well-being; negative relationships leave you feeling anxious and depressed. When you receive support from friends and family, your orbital frontal cortex and mirror neurons are activated, and you experience less anxiety and better mental health. This is why you don't want to isolate yourself when you're anxious. It helps you to spend time with family and friends.

TAMING YOUR AMYGDALA

Remember that your left frontal lobe is associated with positive feelings and action, and your right frontal lobe is associated with negative feelings and withdrawal. If you're like many people who suffer from anxiety, you *underactivate* your left frontal lobe and *overactivate* your right frontal lobe. Withdrawal overactivates your right frontal lobe and your amygdala, which makes your anxiety worse.

When you isolate yourself, you don't get the benefit of activating the orbital frontal areas and mirror neurons that help you control your emotions. Also, when you form intimate relationships, you activate the release of soothing neurochemicals, such as oxytocin. Higher oxytocin levels help blunt pain and help you feel comforted by other people.

To conquer anxiety, you need to activate your left frontal lobe. Because your left frontal lobe has language skills that your right frontal lobe does not, it makes labeling sensations with words ("this is nothing to be worried about") an important part of overcoming anxiety. Its language ability allows you to label your experiences realistically, while activating your left frontal lobe and the positive emotions associated with it.

Your left frontal lobe and your orbital frontal cortex can shut down the HPA axis and the fight-or-flight response. This happens when you activate your left frontal lobe by labeling a situation from a realistic perspective, then take action by doing something positive. In other words, you label a false alarm for what it is—nothing to worry about—then you go ahead and expose yourself to the thing you feared, such as crossing a bridge or talking to strangers. Using this system, you can learn to tame your amygdala.

Patrick Tames His Amygdala

Patrick, a county clerk, experienced chronic free-floating anxiety and periodic panic attacks when he had to deal with the public. He did everything he could to try to keep his anxiety "under wraps." For example, he never volunteered for extra assignments, especially if they involved interacting with others. He spoke only when spoken to, and, even when asked his opinion, he would often say, "Oh, I don't really know."

Patrick was overactivating his right frontal lobe with his passive and withdrawal behaviors. Consequently, his feelings of being overwhelmed and the negative emotions associated with his right frontal lobe were increasing. His passive behavior had allowed his amygdala to be hijacked, putting his frontal lobes into a hypervigilant state about any potential anxiety. Patrick needed to expose himself to fear-producing situations, so that his amygdala could become reconditioned to lessen its over-reactivity. This took repetition and consistency.

He started by visiting the break room at work to make small talk with the people he'd been working with for years but had always avoided. Day after day, despite not "feeling comfortable," he kept showing up in the break room and even managed to strike up some conversations. Next, he started forcing himself to make small talk with the public. The more he practiced making conversation, the easier it became.

Eventually, despite his fear of taking action, Patrick began to volunteer for assignments, especially those that involved interacting with others. He learned to be more competent in dealing with the public and simultaneously felt less anxiety.

You, too, can tame your amygdala, by breaking old habits, such as anxiety, and establishing new habits. This is possible because your brain is capable of establishing new circuits and essentially rewiring itself. To understand how this happens, let's take a closer look at what happens in your brain.

HOW YOUR BRAIN CREATES NEW HABITS

The 100 billion neurons contained in your brain's lobes, hemispheres, hippocampus, and amygdala are not hardwired; they're "softwired," which means they can be rewired. Your neurons have the ability to make new connections with one another. Each neuron is capable of maintaining connections with about 10,000 other neurons. Those connections change as you learn things, such as how to become relaxed, instead of anxious.

Your neurons communicate by sending chemical messengers called neurotransmitters to one another across a gap called a synapse. This transmission is how one neuron gets another neuron to fire. You have more than 100 types of neurotransmitters in your brain.

Some, such as epinephrine, make you anxious, and some, including GABA and serotonin, calm you down. You want the neurotransmitters GABA and serotonin to work more efficiently in your brain, because they promote calmness and a better mood.

The synapses between your neurons also can change to make you less anxious. This ability to change is called *neuroplasticity*. Neuroplasticity makes learning new habits possible. Your brain changes its synapses when you learn something new, including how to be calmer.

The phrase "cells that fire together, wire together" describes how your brain reorganizes itself through neuroplasticity as you learn new things. The more frequently the new connections between your neurons fire together, the higher the chance they will fire together in the future and produce calmness instead of nervousness. They are "wired together," because you are strengthening these new connections. This is the brain-based explanation for how habits get formed and how you can alternatively modify those habits.

The more you practice something, the more likely you are to do it in the future. In other words, the more you practice feeling relaxed, the more likely you are to feel relaxed in general. The same process applies to the anxiety techniques in this book. Neuroplasticity occurs when you do something over and over again. In other words, repetition rewires your brain and creates habits.

However, creating new habits requires effort. When water runs downhill, for example, it's following the path of least resistance. Your brain does this, too—it does what it is used to doing. If you want to create a new habit, one your brain isn't familiar with, you need to make a strong effort to *do what you don't feel like doing*—and then keep doing it. Eventually, you'll find yourself doing it without the effort. It will have become a habit. In other words, if you practice feeling relaxed, instead of feeling anxious, you'll feel relaxed more often than anxious. Likewise, if you practice putting yourself in situations that once triggered anxiety, you will eventually respond to them without anxiety. This is possible because you can decide to override the overactivity of your amygdala. The more you practice the techniques in this book, the calmer you'll be.

I've introduced a fair amount of information about your brain in this chapter. Here are a few critical points that are important to remember:

- Your brain is a complex organ that can change through neuroplasticity.
- If you continue to do what comes easily for you, your anxiety will continue.
- To conquer anxiety, you need to do what you don't feel like doing.
- Because your implicit memory systems and your amygdala can't change on a dime, you need to repeat the skills that you learn in the book over and over again to establish new habits.

Chapter 4
Change Your Diet to Tune Up Your Brain

To ensure that your brain is capable of learning the techniques detailed in the rest of the book, your biochemistry needs to be kept at its optimum.

In this chapter, you'll learn how to provide your brain with the correct building blocks (known as amino acid precursors) to produce the neurotransmitters that calm you down. These amino acid precursors are found in many foods.

GETTING THE RIGHT BRAIN FOOD

Your diet can make you feel worse. It can also make you feel better. What you eat has a major effect on your biochemistry and how your brain functions. Your brain is the highest energy consumer of any organ in your body, and changes in your diet can have a major impact on its ability to function properly. A proper diet provides a good foundation for learning anxiety-reduction techniques.

What you eat can either calm you down or make you feel nervous. Foods loaded with sugar and white flour can make you feel nervous and tense a few hours after you eat them. Foods loaded with fiber and the necessary vitamins and minerals to provide the amino acids your body needs can help you stay calm.

The amino acids found in various foods are crucial building blocks for your brain's neurotransmitters. Your body manufactures these neurotransmitters by synthesizing specific amino acids in the foods you eat. For example, L-glutamine is an amino acid found in foods such as almonds and peaches, and when digested, your body uses it to synthesize into the neurotransmitter GABA. GABA, as we know, helps you stay calm.

The following chart lists some amino acid precursors, their associated neurotransmitters, and a sample of the foods that contain them.

AMINO ACIDS AND SOME FOODS THAT CONTAIN THEM

AMINO ACID PRECURSOR	NEURO-TRANSMITTER	EFFECTS	FOODS
L-tryptophan	serotonin	improves sleep, calmness, and mood	turkey milk shredded wheat pumpkin seeds cottage cheese almonds soybeans
L-glutamine	GABA	decreases tension and irritability, increases calmness	eggs peaches grape juice avocado sunflowers granola peas
tyrosine	dopamine	increases feelings of pleasure	beef fish oats wheat dairy products chicken soybeans
L-phenylalanine	norepinephrine	increases energy and feelings of pleasure and aids memory	peanuts lima beans sesame seeds chicken yogurt milk soybeans

Do you have to remember all these amino acids and their associated neuro-transmitters? No. But you *do* want to eat a balanced meal a least three times a day. By eating three balanced meals per day, you'll likely consume enough of the essential amino acids necessary to minimize your anxiety. Each meal should contain:

- fruit and/or vegetables
- complex carbohydrates (such as whole grains)
- protein

A turkey sandwich on whole wheat bread with carrots and a piece of fruit is a balanced meal. So is rice, fish, and a salad. A bowl of cereal with milk and strawberries is also a balanced meal. You can put many combinations together to create a balanced meal.

 Use this worksheet to chart your progress. Simply check the box for each balanced meal you eat.

BALANCED MEAL WORKSHEET

DAY	BREAKFAST FRUIT/VEG, PROTEIN, CARB	LUNCH FRUIT/VEG, PROTEIN, CARB	DINNER FRUIT/VEG, PROTEIN, CARB
Sunday			
Monday			
Tuesday			
Wednesday			
Thursday			
Friday			
Saturday			
Sunday			
Monday			
Tuesday			
Wednesday			
Thursday			
Friday			
Saturday			
Sunday			
Monday			
Tuesday			
Wednesday			
Thursday			
Friday			
Saturday			

Omega-3 Fatty Acids

Omega-3 fatty acids are also critical for healthy cells (including brain cells). However, your body does not manufacture these essential fatty acids naturally, so you need to include them in your diet. One of the best sources of omega-3 fatty acids is cold-water fish, such as salmon, tuna, and sardines. If you don't consume enough fish, be sure to get your omega-3 fatty acids from other sources, such as canola oil, walnuts, and flaxseed. For the health of your brain, as well as the rest of your body, I recommend taking a daily omega-3 capsule.

Vitamins and Minerals

Vitamins also have a direct effect on your brain chemistry. The B vitamins, in particular, influence the manufacture of specific neurotransmitters. For example, B_6 is needed for the manufacture of dopamine through the amino acids l-phenylalanine and tyrosine. Thiamin (B_1) is needed for GABA synthesis. It is a good policy to eat foods rich in these elements and, if necessary, use vitamin supplements.

Vitamins are not only important as building blocks for some neurotransmitters and your body, but when deprived of them, you can also experience specific deficits in your ability to think clearly. When you add anxiety to the mix, you make matters worse, because stress depletes your supply of B and C vitamins as well as potassium.

Here is a list of foods that are natural sources of B vitamins. In the accompanying chart, you will find some of the major consequences of B-vitamin deficiencies.

FOODS RICH IN B VITAMINS

B_1	B_2	B_6	B_{12}	FOLIC ACID
oatmeal	liver	wheat germ	eggs	carrots
peanuts	cheese	cantaloupe	liver	dark leafy
bran	fish	cabbage	milk	vegetables
wheat	milk	beef	beef	cantaloupe
vegetables	eggs	liver	cheese	whole wheat
brewer's yeast	brewer's yeast	whole grains	kidneys	

B-VITAMIN DEFICIENCIES

LOW B_1	LOW B_2	LOW B_6	LOW B_{12}	LOW FOLIC ACID
decreased alertness	trembling	nervousness	mental sluggishness	memory problems
fatigue	sluggishness	irritability	confusion	irritability
emotional instability	tension	depression	psychosis	mental sluggishness
decreased reaction	depression	muscle weakness	stammering	
time	eye problems	headaches	limb weakness	
	stress	muscle tingling		

Vitamin C.   Vitamin C enhances the immune system and promotes health from infection, disease, and injury. It also helps the adrenal glands. Your adrenal glands (when properly functioning) help you cope with stress. Good food sources of vitamin C include:

- parsley
- broccoli
- bell peppers

- strawberries
- oranges
- lemon juice

- papayas
- cauliflower
- kale

- mustard greens
- Brussels sprouts

Calcium and Magnesium. Calcium and magnesium are also important to prevent tension. They tend to help relax a tense and overwrought nervous system. Calcium is a natural tranquilizer, and magnesium helps relieve anxiety, tension, nervousness, muscular spasms, and tics. Good sources of calcium in foods are:

- dairy products, such as milk, yogurt, and cheese
- canned salmon (especially the bones)
- oysters
- black beans
- mustard greens
- navy beans
- cooked soybeans

- cooked spinach
- tofu
- almonds
- bok choy
- corn tortillas
- calcium-fortified foods, such as fortified orange juice, cereals, waffles, and soymilk

Potassium. Potassium balances the acid-to-alkaline ratio in your system, transmits electrical signals between cells and nerves, and even enhances your athletic performance. It works with sodium to regulate your body's water balance and is necessary for muscle function, energy storage, nerve stability, enzyme and hormone production, and your heart's health against hypertension and stroke. If you take blood pressure medication, you're vulnerable to potassium deficiency. Potassium helps oxygenate your brain for clear thinking. Stress, hypoglycemia, and acute anxiety or depression can result in potassium deficiency. Good food and herb sources of potassium are:

- fresh fruits, especially kiwis and bananas
- potatoes
- parsley
- chile peppers
- sea vegetables
- vegetable broth
- spices and herbs, such as coriander, cumin, basil, ginger, dillweed, tarragon, paprika, and turmeric

- lean poultry and fish
- dairy foods
- legumes and seeds
- whole grains

Vitamin Supplements

Vitamin supplements are just that, supplements. They are not meant to replace good, nutritious food. Consider your diet, not vitamin supplements, the foundation of your health. There is no replacement for a healthy diet. However, sometimes additional vitamin supplements can be helpful, even if you do practice healthy eating habits. I recommend a full-spectrum, once-a-day multivitamin and a daily omega-3 capsule. Include a calcium supplement if you are lactose-intolerant and take magnesium at the same time. Taking a calcium-magnesium supplement (and/or drinking warm milk) before bed improves sleep.

Staying Hydrated

Many people do not realize how important it is to stay hydrated. Your body is 80 percent water. In fact, you can survive without food longer than you can without water. Each day, you lose about 4 percent of your body weight in water through perspiring, urinating, defecating, and even breathing. If you don't replace that water, your body will set off warning signals in the form of anxiety-provoking sensations. Well after your throat gets dry and you feel thirsty, you'll probably get a headache. Then your temperature will begin to rise, you will breathe faster, and your pulse will quicken. If you don't drink water, you'll soon become dizzy, your tongue will swell, and your muscles will spasm. Beyond this point, you're in very dangerous territory. Generally speaking, be sure to drink approximately six 10-ounce (295-ml) glasses of liquid (including juices, milk, and other noncaffeinated drinks) per day.

Peggy Changes Her Diet to Change Her Brain Chemistry

Peggy came to see me because she was tired of suffering from free-floating anxiety and periodic panic attacks. I discovered that she was not only skipping breakfast but often skipped lunch, too, in an effort to keep her weight down. Instead of eating balanced meals, she drank a diet supplement and took a multivitamin as "further assurance" that she was getting all her vitamins. Peggy's remaining meals were composed of processed foods and simple carbohydrates, such as macaroni and cheese, white bread, and frozen, prepackaged dinners. Not surprisingly, she was plagued by low energy and anxiety. She also had difficulty concentrating, and her short-term memory was poor.

I suggested that Peggy start her recovery by ensuring that she ate at least three balanced meals per day. I explained that supplements were no substitute for food, and that a balanced diet would provide her with the essential amino acids needed for a well-functioning brain. I also explained that going for extended periods of time without eating (in essence, fasting) was not helpful for weight loss, because the lack of food was fooling her body into "believing" that it was in a pre-starvation mode, causing it to store fat cells.

Going without meals was also starving her brain, which wasn't getting the fuel it needed to function. To create a solid foundation from which to build her anxiety-reduction skills, Peggy needed to provide her brain with the right foods to produce the essential neurochemistry. This required that she eat at least three balanced meals per day.

Getting started on this new diet wasn't easy for Peggy. Eating in the morning initially made her nauseous, and complex carbohydrates tasted "strange" to her, she said, after a diet of simple carbs. But she adapted and eventually reported being calmer and having more energy. Once Peggy had achieved this solid foundation, she was able to move on to learning anxiety-reduction skills.

A poor diet has long been associated with contributing to health problems, such as diabetes and heart disease. Health problems can make calming your anxiety difficult. The combination of poor diet and health problems thwarts your ability to absorb the important vitamins and minerals that help you form a foundation for overcoming anxiety. If you have health problems, such as diabetes, cardiovascular problems, or an autoimmune disease, you'll need to be impeccable about maintaining a balanced diet.

A balanced diet is critical for providing the optimum brain chemistry needed to develop your anxiety-reduction skills. Without a balanced diet, the anxiety-reduction skills you develop will fall apart like a house of cards.

SUBSTANCES THAT NEGATIVELY AFFECT YOUR BRAIN CHEMISTRY

Now that you know what to eat to build a good foundation, you'll want to know how to avoid creating cracks in that foundation. Some bad habits can create very large cracks in that foundation.

Sugar Highs and Lows

For your brain to function, it also needs food, in the form of glucose (a type of sugar). It derives this glucose when the food you eat is digested. When you eat a balanced diet, your brain receives the proper amount of glucose to provide energy, thought-processing, and a stable mood.

An excess amount of simple sugar in your bloodstream, however, can destabilize moods and cause tension and anxiety. When you consume a lot of simple carbohydrates and sugar-laden foods, such as candy, soda, and fast foods, you unknowingly make your anxiety worse. Although they can make you feel energized in the short term, you pay a high price for that momentary boost of energy.

Here's what happens: When you eat a well-balanced meal containing protein and complex carbs, your digestive system converts the carbohydrates *slowly* into glucose, which is released into the bloodstream and causes your blood-glucose levels to rise. Your pancreas responds to the increase by releasing insulin to help your cells take up the glucose and fuel your brain.

When you consume a high-sugar food, however, the simple carbohydrates are converted to glucose *quickly*. The sudden, excessive increase, or spike, in your blood glucose causes your energy level to soar, and you feel a "sugar high." The high doesn't last long, however; in response to the excessive amount of glucose, your pancreas releases a lot of insulin into the bloodstream to counterbalance the glucose. This causes an energy dip, or crash—but your energy level drops to a point that is lower than it was *before* you consumed the sugar. Worse, the crash is accompanied by feelings of nervousness.

Simple carbohydrates, such as sugar, have no nutritional value; they provide no minerals, vitamins, or enzymes. Sugar steals nutrients, such as the B vitamins, from your body, and B-vitamin deficiencies can cause anxiety. When you eat sugary foods, you'll not only feel anxious, but you will also tend to be irritable and find it difficult to concentrate. Over the years, I've seen many people in my practice who binged on high-sugar foods, such as cookies and candy bars. Not surprisingly, they had difficultly sleeping and were plagued by anxiety. Once they learned about the ill effects of sugar, they quit eating it and felt better.

In addition to its white granulated form, sugar is found in many foods disguised under other names. Check the labels of the foods you eat for the following types of sugars:

- brown sugar
- corn sweeteners
- fructose
- fruit-juice concentrate
- glucose (dextrose)
- high-fructose corn syrup
- honey
- lactose
- maltose
- molasses
- sugar cane juice
- syrup

It pays to check food labels. Many fruit juices are actually loaded with high-fructose corn syrup. To increase your awareness of your sugar intake, note the amount of sugar—of all types, including those on the list above—you consume.

How Much Sugar Is in Your Diet?

For one week, check the Nutritional Facts label for sugar content and add up in the chart (on the following page) the number of grams of sugar you consume daily. You might be surprised by just how much sugar, in all its forms, you consume. If your added sugar intake is more than 24 grams a day, it's too high.

SUGAR AWARENESS WORKSHEET

SUN	MON	TUE	WED	THU	FRI	SAT

Hypoglycemia

If, like Peggy, you go for long periods without eating, your blood sugar can drop too much, a condition known as hypoglycemia. If your blood sugar drops below 50 milligrams per milliliter, you can experience anxiety, shakiness, lightheadedness, irritability, rapid heartbeat, and difficulty concentrating. These symptoms can occur three hours after your last meal. To make matters worse, if you have hypoglycemia and consume sugar-loaded candy bars or soft drinks three hours after eating a meal, the symptoms of anxiety intensify. If you have hypoglycemia, work with a nutritionist to adjust your diet. You can help keep your blood sugar level stable by eating several small meals per day.

Lick the Salt Habit

Consuming excessive amounts of sodium (salt) can make coping with anxiety more difficult. Excessive sodium depletes your body of potassium, and low potassium levels contribute to an increase in anxiety. Sodium can also exacerbate hypertension. It causes fluid retention, which raises your blood pressure, putting stress on your heart and circulatory system. High blood pressure contributes to feelings of "being on edge."

Most people are not aware of the amount of sodium they consume. You don't need to become obsessive about your sodium intake, but because it can contribute to anxiety, you do want to be aware of it. Excessive sodium is found in many foods, including the following:

- canned soups
- canned vegetables
- fast foods
- salted chips
- soy sauce
- salted popcorn

- ketchup (also high in sugar)
- salted nuts
- processed foods
- pickled foods
- restaurant foods
- French fries

How Much Sodium Is in Your Diet?

As an awareness exercise, use the following worksheet to monitor your sodium consumption. As you did in the previous exercise, check Nutrition Facts labels and note, for one week, the number of grams of sodium you consume daily. Aim for a consumption level of no more than 1,500 to 2,300 milligrams a day (less if you are older than fifty).

SODIUM AWARENESS WORKSHEET

SUN	MON	TUE	WED	THU	FRI	SAT

Just Say No to Caffeine

If you're like many people, when you feel worn down and need a "boost," you reach for something to give you enough energy to get through the day. More than likely, what you reach for contains caffeine. Caffeinated drinks such as coffee, energy drinks, and soda can give you a momentary boost, but you can quickly discover that the negatives outweigh the benefits. Caffeine depletes B vitamins, especially thiamin, which is needed for the synthesis of GABA. Caffeine also raises stress hormones. Excessive caffeine puts your body into a prolonged state of stress and hyperalertness. Consuming large amounts of caffeinated drinks is like drinking liquid anxiety.

The *Diagnostic and Statistical Manual of Mental Disorders* (DSM-5™) used by mental health professionals now includes a diagnostic category called *Caffeine Use Disorder*. If you consume more than 250 milligrams of caffeine (the equivalent of two to three cups of brewed coffee) a day, you can experience a wide range of symptoms:

- nervousness
- flushed face
- frequent need to urinate
- muscle twitching
- rapid heartbeat
- diarrhea
- insomnia

- fatigue a few hours after consuming
- restlessness
- panic attacks
- stomach pain
- rapid heartbeat
- ringing in the ears
- trembling

Caffeine raises the levels of the activating neurotransmitters dopamine and norepinephrine, which is closely related to adrenaline. When you consume a lot of caffeine, you can feel adrenaline-charged. Conversely, caffeine dampens levels of adenosine, a neurotransmitter that helps you calm down and become sedated. Chemically shaped like adenosine, caffeine sits on adenosine's receptor site in your brain and blocks its absorption.

There's more bad news. High levels of caffeine, especially if consumed in the afternoon or evening, can cause insomnia or, at the very least, poor sleep quality. Caffeine suppresses Stage 4 sleep, the deepest and most restful stage of sleep. As you will learn in the next chapter, Stage 4 sleep recharges your immune system; if you don't get enough Stage 4 sleep, you not only wake up feeling less rested, but you also become more susceptible to colds. Caffeine also suppresses Rapid Eye Movement (REM), or "dreaming," sleep, and suppressed REM sleep contributes to increased irritability and difficulty concentrating.

The Coffee Addiction

Drinking coffee on an empty stomach in the morning also creates a variety of problems. Skipping breakfast can make you anxious; drinking caffeine on an empty stomach can intensify this anxiety. Despite the initial spurt of energy from the coffee, one to two hours after drinking it, you'll crash and will probably have more difficulty concentrating than if you had eaten breakfast. You'll be tired and will probably experience free-floating anxiety. Because you took in no nutrition at breakfast, you had nothing to provide you with sustained energy and wore yourself out with the caffeine rush. After the crash, you will probably experience headaches, fatigue, and difficulty concentrating.

If you drink a lot of coffee, overcoming anxiety will probably be difficult. Caffeine compromises your ability to calm yourself. If you experience anxiety symptoms from drinking caffeinated coffee, you'll want to cut back or even eliminate it from your diet.

A word of warning: Quitting cold turkey when you're used to consuming a lot of caffeine will bring on headaches and fatigue. This is called caffeine withdrawal. Be sure to cut down slowly, so those symptoms will be gradual. Exercising can help lessen the withdrawal symptoms.

Sources of Caffeine

Caffeine is found in many sources in addition to coffee. One of the most common sources are soft drinks, in particular, colas and other drinks specifically designed to boost your energy levels. These drinks can have as many as ten to twelve teaspoons (50 to 60 grams) of sugar in one can. So you not only get the buzz and drop-off from the caffeine, you experience the added crash from the sugar. If you consume a lot of caffeine and sugar and don't eat three balanced meals a day, count on even more free-floating anxiety and fatigue. This can be a vicious cycle, because you may feel that you need more sugar and caffeine to boost your energy.

You'll also find caffeine in some medications. I have seen people in my practice who have taken medications at night and found that they not only had insomnia, but they also then became anxious because they couldn't sleep.

Jane Cuts the Caffeine and Is Energized

Jane came to my anxiety class because she felt anxious and tense all the time. She typically raced off to work early in the morning without eating breakfast, then ordered a double latte from the coffee cart. At times, she skipped lunch, too. By late afternoon, she was exhausted and went back to the cart for another latte. By that time, she usually felt a little hungry, so she grabbed a muffin.

Not surprisingly, Jane had difficulty concentrating and was filled with anxiety throughout the day. By evening, she felt drained of energy. Unfortunately, this fatigue didn't contribute to sedation at bedtime—Jane also suffered from insomnia.

The first step was to get Jane to improve her diet, so we could determine whether poor diet caused her anxiety symptoms or simply made them worse. She was initially quite resistant to a change in diet, so I explained that her brain needed the right biochemistry to prepare it for learning how to conquer anxiety. In other words, before we could call in the fire department, she had to stop pouring gasoline on the fire. Eventually, Jane did begin to eat balanced meals. It was harder for her to give up the lattes, however; she claimed she needed them for energy.

CAFFEINE CONTENT IN VARIOUS SOURCES

SOURCES	AMOUNT IN MILLIGRAMS
Coffee (8 ounces [235 ml])	
Drip (depending on the bean and to what degree it is roasted)	88–280
Percolated	27–64
Decaffeinated	1.6–13
Tea (one cup)	
Black	45–78
Green	24–56
Oolong	20–64
Darjeeling	45–56
Instant	40–58
Soft Drinks (12 ounces [355 ml])	
Jolt Cola	70
Mountain Dew	55
Coca-Cola	30–45
Dr. Pepper	30–45
Chocolate	
Dark (1 ounce [28 grams])	20
Milk (1 ounce [28 grams])	6–7
Cocoa (5 ounces [140 grams])	4

SOURCES	AMOUNT IN MILLIGRAMS
Medications	
Anacin	32
Appedrine	100
Aqua-Ban	100
Aqua-Ban Max	200
Aspirine	3
Bromo-Seltzer	32
Cafergot	100
Cope	32
Coryban-D	30
Darvon	32.4
Dexatrim	200
Dietac	200
Dristan Decongestant	16.2
Duradyne-Forte	30
Empirin	32
Excedrin	65
Fiorinal	40
Midol	32
Migral	50
NoDoz	32
Soma Compound	32
Vanquish	32
Vivarin	200

I finally convinced her to cut back on the caffeine and take walks in the late afternoon. To Jane's surprise, she eventually felt energized and calm at the same time.

Anxiety in a Bottle

It's a common scenario: You come home from work after a bad day and pour yourself a glass of wine to calm down. But here's the bad news: Anxiety symptoms often *increase* when you try to calm yourself by drinking alcohol. Even though you feel relaxed afterward, in the long run, alcohol works against you. Over the years, I have had many people come in complaining about panic attacks and anxiety and discover that their anxiety is fueled by alcohol.

There are many myths about the beneficial effects of alcohol. If you accept one or more of these myths as truth, expect problems. Although you might believe that alcohol helps you deal with anxiety, the fact is, it actually contributes to it. And alcohol can cause problems for as much as several days after your last drink. Following are some of the most common alcohol myths.

Myth: Alcohol decreases anxiety.

Fact: Alcohol *increases anxiety,* because it lowers GABA.

It is quite common for people to have panic attacks precipitated by recent alcohol use.

Myth: Alcohol decreases stress.

Fact: Alcohol *increases stress,* because it lowers the levels of neurotransmitters that can help you calm down and deal with stress.

Myth: Alcohol lifts you out of depression.

Fact: Alcohol actually *increases depression* by lowering the levels of the neurotransmitter serotonin for as much as a few weeks after the last drink. Low serotonin causes depression.

Myth: Alcohol is a sleep aid.

Fact: Alcohol *destroys deep sleep.* It is common for people to have alcohol-related insomnia during the mid-sleep cycle. Alcohol also dampens your deep and REM sleep.

Physiological Effects of Alcohol

Alcohol is toxic to your brain.   It lowers blood flow to your brain. It also impairs your brain chemistry by degrading the operation of your neurotransmitters. This means that you'll produce fewer of the neurotransmitters that you'll need to stay calm and focused.

The degradation of your neurotransmitters causes numerous emotional and thinking problems. This is because alcohol causes your brain to lower the production of neurotransmitters such as serotonin and GABA. This means that, for at least two weeks after your last drink, serotonin and GABA levels are less available. Low levels of serotonin and GABA are correlated with depression and increased anxiety.

Other neurotransmitters are also lowered as a result of drinking alcohol. Dopamine levels drop, resulting in fewer feelings of pleasure and motivation. Norepinephrine levels fall, resulting in a decreased ability to think clearly and remember. Alcohol also depresses neuropeptides, the brain opiates that include endorphins, in turn depressing your immune system and causing you to be more susceptible to viruses and other illnesses. Finally, if you are suffering from chronic pain connected to an injury, the intensity of your pain will increase over the long term, even though you may feel temporary relief after a drink.

Alcohol damages the hippocampus.   The hippocampus is critically important in the processes of learning and laying down memories. The hippocampus is also the site-specific target for stress hormones, such as cortisol. Too much cortisol in your brain can have a neurotoxic effect on your hippocampus. Alcohol activates the hypothalamic-pituitary-adrenal (HPA) axis and elevates cortisol, actually activating the stress response. In other words, though having a drink feels initially like you are "mellowing out," you are actually raising the levels of stress hormones.

Alcohol increases anxiety.   Having a drink can relax you for a few hours, but in the following days after your drink, you are apt to experience more anxiety than if you hadn't had a drink at all. I have seen countless people who developed an anxiety disorder as a result of their alcohol consumption. The irony is that they were suffering from the belief that they were calming themselves down.

Frieda Exchanges Alcohol for Sleep

Shortly after taking on a new job, Frieda started drinking wine at night to "relax" because she was feeling anxious. She soon began to experience problems with sleep, waking up in the middle of the night and having difficulty getting back to sleep. Even worse, her anxiety increased. Soon, she began to have anxiety attacks. That's when she came to see me. Frieda was suffering from a type of insomnia called mid-sleep cycle awakening or middle insomnia, a typical symptom of alcohol consumption in the evening. After I advised her to quit drinking, not only did her sleep improve, but she also had fewer panic attacks, despite the continued job stress.

Alcohol impairs sleep.   If you drink a "nightcap," you experience shallower sleep than you normally do. Alcohol depresses Stage 4 sleep (the deepest sleep), which recharges your immune system and provides you with the most rest, because stress hormones, such as cortisol, rise after the alcohol wears off. Alcohol also dampens Rapid Eye Movement (REM) sleep, your dream sleep. Drinking at night not only results in losing the opportunity to get a deep sleep; it distorts your dreams and can cause you to wake up in the middle of the night.

Alcohol contributes to a poor diet.   Alcohol can comprise as much as 50 percent of your total daily caloric intake, suppressing your desire to consume macronutrients—fats, carbohydrates, and proteins.

Psychological Effects of Alcohol

Alcohol narrows your perspective.   From a psychological point of view, alcohol leads to "cognitive constriction," which means your capacity to think broadly withers away. The damage alcohol does to the dendrites of your neurons results in less input from other neurons, and you become more prone to black-and-white frames of reference, rather than appreciating the shades of gray. You become less able to deal with the complexities of interpersonal experience.

Alcohol narrows your focus to rigid black-and-white frames of reference (usually black), when you need to develop a broad perspective about your life, which has many dimensions. You want to be mentally flexible and adaptive. In other words, you need shock absorbers to roll with the bumps on the road, not a rigid suspension that can break an axle. This narrow focus causes your hypervigilance and social withdrawal to become worse.

Alcohol pushes your emotions to the extreme.   Alcohol contributes to "affective constriction" by making you more negatively reactive. In other words, you feel emotions in extremes—either very bad or very good, but not in between. Extreme emotions cause you to be less emotionally flexible to withstand the changing dynamics in your life. By the same token, you will also experience anxiety in extremes, either anxious or not anxious but not in between. You'll tend to be on the anxious side of this polarity because the levels of the neurotransmitters GABA and serotonin will be lower. You can even have panic attacks.

Jake Exchanges Alcohol for Exercise

Jake came in to see me after his wife complained about his irritability, poor sleep, and panic attacks. He said that he drank "a few beers" in the evening to "chill out" after a rough day at work. He complained that he felt nervous and anxious during the day and recently had experienced an increased number of panic attacks. When I asked him to describe his day and why he felt so tense, he used language in the extremes; things were either good or bad, and usually bad. Because of his negative perspective, it was difficult for him to articulate why things were so stressful at work and at home.

Jake's ability to maintain attention seemed subtly impaired. Though his condition was not severe enough to warrant a diagnosis of Attention Deficit Disorder (ADD), he easily forgot what he was saying as he jumped from subject to subject. He complained of being sleep-deprived because he woke up in the middle of the night and couldn't get back to sleep.

My first suggestion was that he stop drinking beer at night. His response was, "How am I supposed to unwind?" I told him about the ill effects of alcohol and that instead of unwinding, he was actually "winding himself up" well after his last drink because the alcohol was changing his neurochemistry. I suggested that he unwind by taking a long walk after dinner with his wife. Within two weeks, Jake reported that his sleep had improved, he felt more positive, and the panic attacks had disappeared.

If you suffer from anxiety, you'll want to stay away from alcohol. It makes no sense to compromise your brain when you need to be building a balanced brain chemistry. You want a good foundation from which to learn the anxiety-reduction techniques described in the following chapters.

Chapter 5
Fine-tuning Your Body

If you're troubled by anxiety, it's absolutely necessary that you exercise, get sufficient sound sleep, and breathe properly. And yet, when you are struggling with anxiety, exercise might be the last thing on your mind. When you're anxious, you're often unable to get to sleep or to stay asleep. When you're anxious, you have a tendency to breathe shallowly.

Getting enough exercise and sleep and knowing how to breathe properly contribute to a fine-tuned body. A relaxed and healthy body forms a solid foundation from which you can learn more quickly the anxiety-reduction techniques introduced in this book.

In this chapter, you'll learn how exercise can calm you, how to get a good night's sleep, and how to breathe to relax. We'll discuss the last technique first because it is fundamental to learning how to relax.

BREATHING TO RELAX

Most people take from nine to sixteen breaths per minute when they are at rest. By contrast, a person experiencing a panic attack can take as many as twenty-seven breaths per minute. When your breathing is accelerated, you can experience many of the symptoms associated with a panic attack, including numbness, tingling, dry mouth, and lightheadedness. When you breathe too fast, the muscles in your abdomen tighten up and your chest cavity becomes constricted.

Shallow breathing and breathing too fast are related. When you breathe shallowly, you also breathe too fast. Some people who come to my class have a tendency to talk very fast and don't give themselves a chance to breathe. As they jump from one sentence to another, they whip themselves up into anxiety. They soon forget the neutral topic they began the conversation with and introduce anxiety-provoking topics.

Your breathing rate can speed up when you experience anxiety. Rapid breathing is not only a symptom of anxiety but also a false alarm for a panic attack. To calm yourself down, you'll need to know how to slow your breathing rate.

Catching Your Breath

Your cardiovascular system includes your respiratory system and your circulatory system. This connection between respiration and circulation is why rapid breathing causes your heart rate to speed up and increase anxiety. If you slow your breathing down, your heart rate will also slow down and you will become more relaxed.

Breathing too fast is referred to as hyperventilation, or "overbreathing." Actual physiological changes occur in your brain and body during hyperventilation. When you overbreathe, you pull in too much oxygen, forcing down the carbon dioxide level in your bloodstream. Because carbon dioxide helps maintain the critical acid base (pH) level in your blood, a lower pH level causes your nerve cells to become more excitable, and you can feel anxiety or associate the feelings with a panic attack.

The excessive dissipation of carbon dioxide leads to hypocapnic alkalosis, which makes your blood more alkaline and less acidic. The alkalinity constricts your blood vessels, so that less blood flows through. And because your blood carries oxygen to your brain, your brain also gets less oxygen. The paradox is that though you are breathing more quickly, too much oxygen is inhaled, and less is available to your tissues.

Hypocapnic alkalosis also causes the blood vessels in your brain to constrict, which leads to dizziness, lightheadedness, and feelings of unreality. You can also experience tingling in the extremities. If you're prone to panic attacks, you tend to over-respond to these physiological sensations and, as a result, breathe even more quickly; you keep the vicious cycle going.

Indeed, hyperventilation is self-perpetuating. It leads to lightheadedness, numbness, dizziness, blurred vision, cold hands, heart palpitations, muscle weakness, difficulty concentrating, and the feeling of not being able to breathe enough air (dyspnea)—the same symptoms experienced in a panic attack. The abnormally sensitive carbon dioxide receptors in your brainstem can read the drop in carbon dioxide as a "false alarm" of suffocation. This dyspnea, the feeling of not getting enough air, can spur a panic attack and even more hyperventilation.

If you have a habitual tendency to hyperventilate, it can carry over into your sleep. Nocturnal panic attacks, which are similar to diurnal (daytime) panic attacks, can be spurred by hyperventilation. When you hyperventilate at night, you activate the same brain systems, experience the same bodily sensations, and have the same tendency to associate these sensations with panic. Your expectations about nighttime panic and your fear that the physiological symptoms will occur during sleep can actually contribute to nighttime panic.

You may feel more anxious and on the verge of panic when you hyperventilate, but you need *not* associate hyperventilation with a panic attack, as you will learn in chapter 6. You can learn to minimize these symptoms. Although breathing retraining is one of the methods of overcoming anxiety, breathing properly can also help you gain a sense of self-confidence and can lead to a sense of being relaxed in general.

Greta Catches Her Breath

I was on call for the emergency room one rainy January night, when my beeper went off. I was called in to see Greta, who lay on a hospital cot still looking bewildered by her experience of two hours earlier. She had called 911 because she thought she was having a heart attack. She told me it all started when she began to hyperventilate. "Soon, it felt like my heart was going to jump out of my chest. It seemed like it was ready to explode."

Greta had had a series of similar episodes but none this severe. "It seemed like each attack was getting worse, and they all started with the breathing problem," she said. "I felt like I was going to suffocate and couldn't get enough air, no matter how hard I tried."

I helped Greta understand that she didn't have a heart problem and that she was suffering from the beginnings of a panic disorder. Because her hyperventilation seemed to be the trigger for her panic symptoms, we started her treatment with the breathing exercises that you will learn in this chapter.

Restructuring Your Breathing

To learn to relax, you'll need to force yourself to develop new habits, such as the way you breathe. Because one of the most common symptoms of panic is shortness of breath, you'll want to learn to breathe differently.

Whenever you feel anxious, stop and note your breathing, then slow it down. Breathing deeply, especially with a longer exhalation, will help you relax. You can shift from the fight-or-flight response (activated by your sympathetic nervous system) to the relaxation response (activated by your parasympathetic nervous system) by using the following methods.

1. Hold your breath for 10 to 15 seconds. This temporarily prevents the dissipation of carbon dioxide.

2. Breathe in and out of a paper bag. You will reinhale the carbon dioxide in the bag and restore the balance of oxygen and carbon dioxide in your bloodstream.

3. Exercise vigorously when you're anxious. This increases your metabolism and produces more energy. The inhaled oxygen is used up by the process of metabolism, and a larger quantity of carbon dioxide will be produced.

4. Practice deep abdominal breathing, which allows your lungs to fill to capacity. This slows your body down.

Breathing Exercises

In this section, you'll learn three different breathing exercises. Learning these will enable you to practice breathing, no matter how little time you have. Each of the following techniques can fit into available windows of time.

When you breathe too fast, the muscles in your abdomen tighten up, and your chest cavity becomes constricted. You want to reverse this by learning to breathe using a method that overemphasizes your diaphragm. This will help you remember how to breathe deeply. As you breathe abdominally, your belly rises when you inhale and drops when you exhale. This is because the diaphragm, the large dome-shaped muscle under your rib cage, expands and contracts. When you inhale, your diaphragm contracts and pulls down, as your abdominal muscles relax. This allows your lower lungs to expand, so that you can breathe deeply. When you exhale, your diaphragm moves back up, and your abdominal muscles contract.

Breathing Exercise 1

1. Lie on your back on a carpeted floor or bed. Put a pillow under your head and two pillows on your belly. This position allows you to watch the pillows rise as you use your diaphragm muscles to breathe. While inhaling, breathe through your nose. Now, take a deep breath and watch the pillows rise. While exhaling, watch the pillows go down.

2. While continuing to lie on your back, set aside the pillows and put your hand on your belly. Use the breathing techniques in step 1 and notice your hand rising and falling with every inhalation and every exhalation.

3. Still lying on your back, place your arms at your side and follow the same breathing method. Notice your belly rise and fall with each inhalation and exhalation.

4. Now, sit on an easy chair or a sofa and watch your belly rise and fall with each inhalation and exhalation.

5. Sit up straight, in an upright chair, and repeat this breathing method. Make sure that your shoulders and chest are still.

6. Finally, stand up and repeat the exercise.

Set aside 15 to 20 minutes to practice Exercise 1 at least once a day. It's best if you practice this exercise in a quiet place where you won't be interrupted. Try to clear your mind of the day's concerns and consider it a break.

You won't be able to practice Exercise 1 on the spur of the moment. However, you will be able to practice an abbreviated version of it.

Breathing Exercise 2
The next exercise can be practiced sitting down and requires only a few minutes.

1. Find a comfortable sitting position.

2. Put both feet on the floor with your arms at your sides.

3. Breathing in, fill your lungs with more air than you usually do.

4. Wait a moment before you exhale.

5. Slowly exhale more air than you think you can.

6. Inhale again and watch your belly rise.

7. Hold for a moment.

8. Exhale slowly.

9. Repeat this several times.

Breathing Exercise 3
Use this exercise to monitor your breathing throughout the day and reestablish a calming breathing pattern.

1. Breathe through your nose.

2. Slow your breathing to eight to twelve breaths per minute. The slower the better.

3. Exhale more slowly than you inhale.

4. After breathing out, hold a moment before taking your next breath.

Try any one of these abdominal breathing exercises the next time you feel anxious. Notice how some of your anxiety drifts away. Practice breathing on a regular basis, and do it often, so that it becomes your habitual way of breathing. Try to stop what you are doing every hour and slow down your breathing by breathing abdominally for at least 30 seconds.

Make copies of this worksheet, so you can check each goal daily, as you accomplish it. By practicing these techniques, you can interrupt your bad habit of breathing shallowly and return to a more relaxing pace of breathing.

YOUR DAILY BREATHING GOALS

GOALS	SUNDAY	MONDAY	TUESDAY	WEDNESDAY	THURSDAY	FRIDAY	SATURDAY
I practiced abdominal breathing every hour during the day.							
I practiced for about 15 minutes around lunch.							
I practiced for about 15 minutes in the evening.							
I reminded myself that to rewire my brain I need to practice these breathing techniques.							

STRETCH AWAY THE TENSION

When you are anxious, and especially if you have GAD, which is characterized by constant worry, you have a tendency to tighten your muscles. A considerable amount of energy is wasted in maintaining muscle tension, which contributes to the fatigue GAD sufferers experience. Suffering from anxiety can make you feel "all wound up." When chronic anxiety builds up in your muscles, the constant muscle tension overdevelops the connective tissue and makes the tendons thicken and shorten. Chronic anxiety also overactivates the sympathetic nervous system (see chapter 3), resulting in tension buildup in an already burdened system. The way to get rid of the buildup of tension is to stretch.

If you have a sedentary lifestyle, you can be vulnerable to tension buildup in your body. Because of your lack of movement, your muscles tighten up and atrophy. The tension that's "stored" in your body contributes to yet more anxiety because your body "feels tense."

To drive out tension and relax your muscles, you need to stretch. Your muscles are endowed with a rich blood supply, and stretching can promote better blood flow to your muscles. When you stretch your muscles, you force used, de-oxygenated blood back into the lungs for refueling. The re-oxygenated blood flows back out to your muscles, refreshing and invigorating them and helping you release tension.

Stretching Exercises

Perform the following simple stretches throughout the day. Some of these stretches can be practiced sitting down or standing. If you lead a sedentary life, I recommend performing at least one of these stretches once an hour. Or, in the middle of the day, try all of them, giving yourself at least a few minutes for each.

Chest Expander

While standing, widen your stance and stretch your arms up and to the side, making the figure of an X, while breathing in deeply. Exhale as you bring your arms back down to your sides.

Neck Roll

While sitting or standing, drop your chin to your chest, then slowly roll your head around 360 degrees. Then roll it in the opposite direction.

Shoulder Shrug

While sitting or standing, raise your shoulders up to your ears. Then roll your shoulders back. Imagine your shoulder blades touching. Next, drop your shoulders. Do this exercise slowly, several times.

Prayer/Hand Push

While standing or sitting, place your hands together in a prayer position close to your chest. With your elbows pointing downward, push both hands together.

You can practice these stretching exercises or find some of your own. Vary the stretches, but practice them often.

MOVE YOUR BODY TO RELAX

Exercise plays a fundamental role in rebalancing your body and your brain and produces a "tranquilizing" effect. This is because physical exertion creates biochemical changes that can dampen your anxiety. Exercise is a far better treatment for anxiety than taking antianxiety medication, and it has none of the negative side effects. In fact, exercise has only positive effects. For example, it enhances oxygenation of your blood. When your blood is transported to your brain, you feel alert and calm. Exercise also lowers the acidity in your body, which increases your energy level.

Following is a list of just some of the many positive benefits of exercise:

- Exercise enhances neurogenesis—new neurons emerge in the hippocampus.
- Exercise lowers pH (increased acidity) of your blood, which increases your energy level.
- Exercise improves circulation (including in your brain).
- Exercise increases oxygenation of your blood and brain, which increases your alertness and ability to concentrate.
- Exercise improves digestion, which helps you make better use of the food you eat.
- Exercise improves elimination from your lungs, skin, and bowels.
- Exercise improves blood-sugar regulation.
- Exercise lowers blood pressure (by lowering hypertension).
- Exercise lowers cholesterol levels.
- Exercise reduces insomnia.
- Exercise helps you lose weight.

Here are some other benefits:

- Exercise reduces muscle tension, which tends to make you feel tense and anxious.
- Exercise rechannels bottled-up frustration, which can contribute to anxiety.

- Exercise increases the metabolism of excess adrenaline and thyroxin (a hormone produced by your thyroid gland), which contribute to hypervigilance and tension, clearing them from your system.

There are many ways to exercise. Some involve a time commitment, while others can be done on the spur of the moment. You can walk or perform an aerobic exercise, such as running or cycling. All of these promote relaxation and a greater sense of well-being.

With aerobic exercise, many people report a "runner's high." This feeling of well-being is the result of the release of your body's endorphins, which are natural brain opiates. Not only do you experience a euphoric and calming feeling after you exercise, but your stress hormones are also reduced.

Often, people have excuses that can keep them from exercising. If they are anxious and feel pressured by a lack of time or energy, the thought of trying to squeeze one more thing, even if it's good for them, into their already crowded day just creates more anxiety. The chart below lists some common excuses for avoiding exercise.

Preparation for a major event, such as a marathon or a bicycle trek, can be great exercise in itself. For example, I've hiked to the bottom of the Grand Canyon, which entails hiking 4,000 to 5,000 feet (1,220 to 1,525 meters) down to the bottom and then back up again, twenty-six times. Sometimes, I hike the 26 miles (42 kilometers) from rim to rim in a day. The point is that I didn't just get up one morning and say to myself, "I think I'll hike the Grand Canyon today." In the months leading up to the big hike, I prepared by hiking the hills near my home with a pack and weights. My wife tells me I look ridiculous, and I probably do, but during that preparation period, I sleep better and generally feel much more relaxed.

Getting good exercise doesn't mean having to join an expensive health club, suit up in expensive workout gear, or run 5 miles a day. Exercise can take any form.

SOLUTIONS TO OVERCOME EXERCISE AVOIDANCE

RATIONALIZATION	SOLUTION
I'm too anxious to exercise.	Exercise calms you down.
I don't have the time.	Break your exercise into 10-minute increments.
I don't belong to a gym.	Run, hike, swim, or play tennis in your neighborhood.
I'm not athletic.	You can walk, cycle, swim, or climb stairs.
I'd rather do something fun that doesn't seem like exercise.	Join a dancing class, garden, or just dance to good music in your living room.
People will see me.	Invest in a treadmill or stationary bicycle and work out in the privacy of your home.
I'm too out of shape.	You'll get into shape by exercising. You can start slowly.
I don't feel like it.	The biggest hurdle is getting started. When you keep at it, it becomes easier. Don't forget about the power of neuroplasticity.

Walking is one of the easiest ways to get exercise, and even strenuous yard work can result in an aerobic boost. If the thought of squeezing another commitment into your day seems overwhelming, start by making small, manageable changes first, such as taking the stairs, instead of the elevator, parking your car at the far end of the parking lot when you shop, or walking to the mailbox or corner store instead of driving. Then work up to a regular routine.

Following is a list of activities that you can do anytime, to incorporate exercise into your daily routine:

- shoveling snow
- raking leaves
- climbing stairs
- vacuuming
- walking to work
- walking the dog
- riding your bicycle

- horseback riding
- jumping on a trampoline
- throwing horseshoes
- jumping rope
- playing volleyball
- shooting baskets

Take a moment to think about the ways you can include exercise in your day, then write them down below. Later, if you find yourself slacking off or becoming bored with your exercise routine, you can come back to this list to keep you motivated.

HOW CAN YOU INCLUDE EXERCISE IN YOUR DAY?

_____   _____

_____   _____

_____   _____

_____   _____

_____   _____

_____   _____

_____   _____

_____   _____

_____   _____

_____   _____

Try to schedule your exercise into your day, so that it is an expectation—a must. One way to ensure that you get regular exercise is to use the following worksheet. Write down the type of exercise you performed, the length of time you engaged in it, and the date. For maximum results, engage in some kind of exercise at least once a day.

It's best if the exercise:

- is regular (four to five times per week).

- is at least twenty to thirty minutes in duration.

- is graduated in intensity (for example, don't run three miles if you have never run— work up to it).

- includes a warm-up and a cool down—stretching works well.

- is aerobic, to get your heart rate up.

 Use this worksheet to monitor the regularity of your exercise. This will help you be more consistent.

EXERCISE WORKSHEET

TYPE OF EXERCISE	LENGTH OF TIME	DATE

SLEEPING ONCE AGAIN

Andre, a teacher, was plagued by free-floating anxiety, tension headaches, sore shoulders, and constant worrying. He also complained of insomnia and the constant feeling that something bad was going to happen. These symptoms started roughly one year before he came to see me and had been steadily increasing in intensity. He came in because he was concerned about becoming irritable with the children in his eighth-grade math class.

Despite complaining that he would have no energy, he complied with my suggestion to cut back on his consumption of caffeine. I then suggested that he exercise to provide himself with a combination of energy and calmness. He needed some convincing.

I told him about the physiology of exercise and what he had to gain. His response was that he didn't have time to exercise. He did admit that after dinner he "kicked back and caught up on email and surfed the 'net. Besides, when am I supposed to unwind?"

With prodding, Andre agreed to try walking for half an hour each evening. After a few weeks of walking, he reported that his sleep had improved and he felt more relaxed. He said, "It's getting so that I resent it when it rains. Walking has become my way of unwinding." He reported a few weeks later that, when it rained, he grabbed an umbrella, "because I know that if I don't get my walk in, I'll feel more pent up the next day."

Like Andre, if you are plagued by anxiety, you likely have sleep problems. When you feel anxious, it is understandably difficult to unwind and sleep. If you suffer from chronic anxiety, your stress hormones do not drop down to normal levels at night. Stress raises your levels of norepinephrine and epinephrine, which activate your nervous system. You can keep yourself tense and anxious by worrying about anything and everything. This free-floating anxiety tends to promote shallow sleep, the result being that you spend less time in the deep stages of sleep, which help boost your immune system.

The Four Stages of Sleep

A normal sleep cycle comprises four stages of sleep. Thanks to instruments such as the electroencephalograph (EEG), which monitors brain waves, we know that sleep stages are represented by different types of brain waves: slow, fast, and dream sleep. Slow-wave sleep is the deepest and most restful; fast-wave is the most shallow and least restful. In dream sleep, your brain waves are fast and your eyes move, which is why this type of sleep is referred to as Rapid Eye Movement (REM) sleep. Although you generally go through REM sleep periods every ninety minutes, most of your REM sleep is packed into the latter portion of your sleep. In contrast, the slowest wave sleep occurs earlier in your sleep cycle.

- **Stage 1 Sleep** Stage 1 sleep is a transition state between waking and sleeping. The brain waves are fast, and if you are awakened from this stage of sleep, you might report that you were not really asleep.

- **Stage 2 Sleep** Stage 2 sleep is also light, with fast brain waves. If you have insomnia, you might complain that you did not sleep, when in fact you were experiencing Stage 2 sleep. You spend half the night in Stage 2 sleep. During periods of increased anxiety, your Stage 2 sleep increases at the expense of deep sleep because of the increase in stress hormones.

- **Stages 3 and 4 Sleep** In sleep Stages 3 and 4, you get your deep sleep, with slow brain waves, referred to as theta and delta waves. Stage 4 is the most important stage of sleep because your immune system gets a boost and your body functions slow down. Anxiety increases the activating neurotransmitters norepinephrine and epinephrine, which dampen your slow-wave sleep. When you are deprived of deep sleep, your immune system is suppressed and your body can ache. This starts a vicious cycle, because the achiness, in turn, prevents you from getting deep sleep. Fortunately, if you are sleep-deprived, the first stage to rebound is deep sleep.

- **Dream Sleep** Dream sleep is not deep sleep. It is called Rapid Eye Movement (REM) sleep because your eyes move, and if you are awoken during this period, you would probably report vivid visual dreams. Most of your body functions operate much like they do during wakefulness. For example, your metabolism during REM sleep is similar to wakefulness, and energizing neurotransmitters are active. You might dream that you are running, and most of your organs function as if you *are* running. The only difference is that you are dreaming, and your limbs are paralyzed.

Practice Good Sleep Hygiene for a Good Night's Sleep

Now that you have a better idea of the types of sleep, you'll learn how to get the deepest sleep. In this section, I'll provide some basic guidelines that fall under the term "sleep hygiene" to help you get the best night's sleep.

Adjust Your Body Clock

Your sleep is affected by the light of day and the dark of night. During the day, light comes in through your eyes, and your retina sends the information to your pineal gland, which is positioned in the middle of your brain. Your pineal gland responds to light by suppressing the production of melatonin, convincing your brain that it is daytime and not the time to become sedated. When it's dark, your retina sends information to your pineal gland that it should produce melatonin to induce sedation.

Because the amount of light you are exposed to during the daytime affects your sleep, you want to maximize your exposure to bright light in the daytime to set your body clock to match the natural day/night cycle of the world around you. At night, you want to do the opposite and minimize your exposure to light, especially if you suffer from insomnia. Avoid using your computer in the late evening, for example. When you look at the computer screen for extended periods of time, you're essentially looking at light. This light tricks your brain into adjusting to a daytime pattern and suppresses your pineal gland's secretion of melatonin, which you need for sleep. To avoid having your body clock, also known as your circadian rhythm, become maladapted to the day/night cycle, be sure to use soft light during the few hours before going to sleep.

Adjust Your Body Temperature

Your circadian rhythm is tied not only to light exposure but also to your body temperature. A warm body temperature leads to a light sleep. Ideally, when you go to sleep at night, your body temperature should be in the process of dropping.

In the morning, just before you rise from bed, your body temperature is on the rise. By getting out of bed and exposing yourself to light, as well as moving your body, you promote a further rise in body temperature. If you're sleep-deprived, you probably feel sluggish when you wake up. However, once you expose yourself to light and move around, your body temperature will rise, and you'll feel better.

If you have insomnia, you might have difficulty regulating your body temperature. Your body temperature can actually increase at night, when it should be going down. This can occur if you fail to get exercise during the day. By making sure that you exercise during the day, you can promote a dip in your body temperature at night.

You can also help lower your body temperature by keeping your bedroom cool at night. If your bedroom is stuffy and warm, open a window. Also, make sure that you don't use too many covers. If you are sweating, throw off a blanket. Stay cool, not hot or cold.

Exercise to Promote Good Sleep

Exercise not only has a calming effect on your body, but it also helps you sleep. Try to exercise three to six hours before bedtime. Exercising in this window helps you sleep better because the exercise elevates your heart rate and body temperature, but there is still enough time for your heart rate and body temperature to drop before you want to sleep. Avoid exercising less than three hours before bed; your heart rate will still be up and your body temperature will be too high. Remember, you want a cool body temperature to promote good sleep.

Maintain the Right Diet for Sleep

Your diet has a major effect on your sleep. If you eat foods rich in tryptophan in the evening, you'll probably become sleepy. Tryptophan is an amino acid that converts to serotonin, which calms you down. Some complex carbohydrates contain tryptophan. Avoid simple carbohydrates such as white bread, which are not helpful. Simple carbohydrates increase the production of tryptophan to serotonin on a short-term basis, and when your blood glucose rises, you can wake up. Choose complex carbohydrates, such as whole wheat bread. When you eat complex carbohydrates, the serotonin conversion occurs on a long-term basis, and a slow and sustained rise in glucose occurs. A glass of warm milk, which contains both tryptophan and calcium, can also make you sleepy.

Vitamins can influence your sleep as well. Deficiencies of B vitamins, calcium, and magnesium may inhibit your sleep. Taking a calcium-magnesium supplement at night can help you relax and help relieve restless leg syndrome.

Keep Your Sound Environment Boring

Your brain is geared to pay attention to novelty, so try to ensure that there are few sounds to grab your attention. Avoid keeping the television on at night; it can periodically grab your attention and wake you up. If your environment is noisy, try using "white noise." It's boring and monotonous and serves as a good screen for other noises, such as barking dogs and passing traffic. Some people keep a fan on all night long to provide white noise. Another useful technique is good-quality earplugs.

Preserve Your Sleep Environment

Make sure that the time you spend in bed is only for sleep or sex. Do not watch television, balance your checkbook, discuss finances with your spouse, or argue in bed. Make your bed carry only one association—sleep.

Practice Relaxation

Practicing relaxation methods during the day helps you sleep at night. Relaxation methods work best if practiced twice daily, once during the day and once before bed. They serve to reduce the effects of stress. Relaxation audiotapes have been shown to be helpful. However, some people complain about the noise the tape player makes when it clicks off. Try to make sure that your tape or CD player can turn itself off without a click, or click it off yourself, so that you remain in control of the process. In the next chapter, I'll discuss relaxation methods, such as imagery, self-hypnosis, and meditation, all of which you can use to help you sleep.

Foods That Help You Sleep

If you have trouble getting to sleep, try including some of the following foods into your evening meals or bedtime snacks:

- brown rice
- a whole wheat bagel
- dairy products, such as milk and cheese
- legumes, such as beans and lentils
- whole grains

Easing into Sleep

If you try too hard to go to sleep, the opposite will happen. Lying there thinking about the fact that you are still awake promotes fast brain waves and the release of epinephrine and norepinephrine, the activating neurotransmitters that increase muscle tension, heart rate, blood pressure, and stress hormones. If you toss and turn for more than one and a half hours after you go to bed, get up and go to another room. By getting out of bed, you allow your body temperature to drop.

Tell yourself that since you are lying in bed anyway, you might as well use the time to relax. You can also use the relaxation methods introduced in the next chapter to quiet your mind. Use this passive effort to promote sleep, instead of *trying* to get to sleep.

Change the Way You Think About Sleep

For a long-term solution to insomnia, use a "cognitive behavioral approach." Identify your false thoughts and replace them with accurate information about sleep. For example, if you wake up in the middle of the night, reframe your wakefulness in one of the following ways:

- If I don't get a good night's sleep tonight, I will tomorrow night.
- This isn't great, but at least I've gotten some sleep.
- I may get back to sleep, I may not. Either way, it is not the end of the world.

By adopting these accurate thoughts about sleep, you take the pressure off yourself and will probably relax enough to get back to sleep.

How Not to Get a Good Night's Sleep

Alcohol Approximately 10 percent of all sleep-maintenance problems (middle insomnia) are caused by alcohol. Alcohol contributes to mid-sleep-cycle awakening, because the alcohol wears off during your sleep. (See chapter 4 for more on how alcohol adversely affects sleep.)

Sleep Aids Avoid using over-the-counter sleep aids, commonly called "sleeping pills." If you use sleeping pills, you may find that, initially, they can help you get to sleep. The downside is that your quality of sleep is poor, and you wake up feeling less rested in the morning. Like alcohol, sleeping pills suppress important stages of sleep. They can also lead to tolerance and withdrawal. In other words, over time, you gradually need more of the drug to get to sleep, and when you try to get to sleep without the medication, you find it harder than if you hadn't used it at all. These sleep problems occur with prescribed medications as well as the over-the-counter types. With respect to sleep medication, less is more.

Chris Uses Good Sleep Hygiene to Improve Her Sleep

Chris was referred to my anxiety class by her primary care physician after he told her that he would no longer prescribe sleep medications for her. He was worried that she was getting dependent on them and thought that her insomnia had to do with anxiety. She did, in fact, acknowledge a chronic undercurrent of anxiety and periodic panic attacks.

A few times, she was awakened at night by panic attacks. Chris began to fear sleeping because the last nocturnal panic attack had been so frightening. She said that she had gotten into a pattern of staying up as late as she could, until she was exhausted enough to get to sleep. This didn't seem to work, however, because her sleep was fitful and she frequently woke up.

When asked how she spent her time between 1:00 and 2:00 AM, she said, "I just catch up on email." I told her about the low light–melatonin link and persuaded her to do her emailing in the morning. I also asked her to take a brisk walk after dinner, then to eat a snack of complex carbohydrates, such as half of a whole wheat bagel, just before bedtime. When Chris admitted to having a glass or two of wine with dinner, I suggested she discontinue drinking and gave her suggestions on how to structure in three balanced meals per day. I also advised her to cut down on her caffeine consumption. After some mild protest, she complied, despite having trouble understanding the connection between skipping breakfast, drinking too much caffeine, and poor sleep hygiene. Once she began to practice these good sleep-hygiene techniques, her sleep gradually improved. And to her delight, she felt less tense and anxious during the day.

Overcoming Chronic Insomnia

There are two types of insomnia: early insomnia and sleep-maintenance insomnia. If you have early insomnia, you have difficulty getting to sleep. Don't worry if you can't get to sleep as soon as you hit the pillow. Few people can get to sleep in less than fifteen minutes. (In fact, if you can get to sleep in under fifteen minutes, you're sleep-deprived.) Most people take from fifteen to twenty minutes to get to sleep. But if it regularly takes you a couple of hours to get to sleep, you have insomnia.

If you have sleep-maintenance insomnia, you have difficulty *staying* asleep. Although you might fall asleep without difficulty, you wake up in the middle of the night and have trouble getting back to sleep. Beware that you can overestimate sleep-maintenance insomnia. Most people wake up from time to time in the middle of the night and go back to sleep relatively quickly. But if it takes you more than an hour and a half to get back to sleep, you probably have sleep-maintenance insomnia.

If you have early insomnia, expose yourself to bright light in the *early* morning. This ensures that melatonin production stays low throughout the day and that your body temperature is lowest when you sleep. If you have sleep-maintenance insomnia, expose yourself to bright light in the *late* morning, so your body temperature is lowest in the middle hours of your sleep cycle and you can stay asleep. Remember that your body temperature needs to be cool at night, so that you can sleep deeply.

Many people who suffer from chronic insomnia try to adjust to the sleep deprivation by doing precisely the wrong things to "catch up." Avoid taking a nap during the day or sleeping longer in the morning to compensate for sleep loss. Those bad habits make it more difficult to sleep the next night.

Sleep Hygiene Guidelines

You don't need a medical sleep study to help you change your sleep pattern. Follow the techniques below to help yourself get better sleep.

1. Cut your caffeine intake, and avoid drinking caffeine on an empty stomach.

2. Be sure to eat three balanced meals a day.

3. Avoid sugar.

4. Don't "try too hard" to go to sleep. You'll frustrate yourself and work yourself into an anxious state of mind. Tell yourself, "It's okay if I get just a few hours of sleep tonight. I will catch up the next night." This change in expectation will free you up to relax and get to sleep. The harder you try to go to sleep, the harder it will be to induce sleep.

5. Don't use your bed for anything but sleep (and sex).

6. If you can't sleep and find yourself tossing and turning, get up and go to another room.

7. Avoid drinking large quantities of liquid at night. This lowers the sleep threshold because you will be prone to waking up to urinate.

8. Avoid bright light for at least a few hours before going to sleep. Don't work on the computer in the late evening.

9. Do all your planning for the next day before you get into bed. If you think of something you need to remember, get up and write it down. Tell yourself that you will postpone thinking or worrying about anything until the next day.

10. Avoid daytime napping. Naps steal sleep from the nighttime.

11. Eat a light snack with complex carbohydrates before bed. Foods rich in L-tryptophan (such as whole grains and warm milk) are advisable. Don't eat anything with sugar or salt before bed.

12. Avoid protein snacks at night; protein blocks the synthesis of serotonin and promotes alertness.

13. Exercise three to six hours before you go to bed. A brisk walk before or after dinner is perfect.

14. If noise bothers you, use earplugs or a white-noise machine.

15. Avoid alcohol.

16. If you are troubled by chronic insomnia, try the sleep scheduling technique (see page 77).

17. Try the relaxation exercises described in the next chapter. These will help you go to sleep or get back to sleep if you wake up during the night.

The Sleep Scheduling Technique

If you suffer from chronic insomnia, try the *sleep scheduling technique.* This technique involves changing your bedtime schedule. By adjusting the time you go to bed, you build up "sleep pressure" (sleepiness) to go to sleep and stay asleep through the night. This technique works because people who are sleep-deprived usually fall asleep earlier the following night to catch up on lost sleep.

The sleep scheduling approach requires that you get up at the same time each morning, despite the amount of sleep you received the previous night. But, instead of going to bed earlier at the end of the day, you go to bed later. You're probably thinking, "I'm sleep-deprived. I need to allow myself as much chance to sleep as possible, even if I toss and turn!" Remember that you are trying to build up sleep pressure.

Here's how it works. Calculate how many hours on average you actually sleep and add one more hour. Use this formula to determine how much sleep time you will allow yourself. For example, if you averaged five hours of sleep a night over the past month, despite staying in bed for eight hours, allow yourself six hours of potential sleep time. If your normal wake-up time is 6:00 AM, go to bed at 11:30 PM.

Do this for at least four weeks. Your goal is to fill up most of the time you spend in bed with sleep. When your body temperature adjusts and the sleep pressure builds, add another hour, to give yourself seven hours to sleep. Work yourself up to eight hours of sleep by adding half hour increments to your potential sleep time.

This approach is useful if you have chronic insomnia, *not* if you have experienced a night or two of poor sleep. If you're a chronic insomniac, you want to rewire your brain to repair your sleep cycle. Remember that changing your habits involves rewiring your brain, and the way you do this is through repetition. You need to stick with these changes, so they can be rewired into your brain. When your sleep cycle is out of synch, sleep scheduling helps it get back into synch. By practicing sleep scheduling, you increase your sleep efficiency.

Chapter 6
Relearning Calmness

Feeling calm may seem like an experience enjoyed by people without anxiety, but not by you. How can they be so blessed? Are they just lucky, or are you cursed? Although it sounds impossible when you are suffering from anxiety, the good news is that you can *learn* to relax and be calm. You have that capacity built into your body.

As you learned in chapter 3, your autonomic nervous system has two branches: the sympathetic nervous system and the parasympathetic nervous system. The sympathetic nervous system activates your body; your parasympathetic nervous system calms it down. In this chapter, you'll relearn to tap into the talents of your parasympathetic nervous system.

Normally, the sympathetic and the parasympathetic nervous systems balance each other out. But when you suffer from anxiety, your sympathetic branch learned to dominate. Too much activation makes you anxious. You want to bring the two branches back into balance. To heal your anxiety, you need tap into the skills of your parasympathetic nervous system, so you can calm down.

Your parasympathetic nervous system has a counterbalance to the fight-or-flight response. Dubbed the *relaxation response* by Harvard professor Herbert Benson, it describes your body's parasympathetic nervous system in action. The relaxation response slows down your breathing and helps lower your heart rate and metabolism.

Notice in the following chart how the relaxation response and the fight-or-flight response balance each other out.

FIGHT-OR-FLIGHT RESPONSE (SYMPATHETIC NERVOUS SYSTEM)	RELAXATION RESPONSE (PARASYMPATHETIC NERVOUS SYSTEM)
↑ Heart rate	↓ Heart rate
↑ Blood pressure	↓ Blood pressure
↑ Metabolism	↓ Metabolism
↑ Muscle tension	↓ Muscle tension
↑ Breathing rate	↓ Breathing rate
↑ Mental arousal	↓ Mental arousal

For thousands of years, people in societies across the globe have developed techniques to induce the relaxation response and activate the parasympathetic nervous system—without knowing of their existence. Referred to as prayer and meditation, these practices were devised to engender spirituality and a sense of inner peace.

Over the past century, a number of practices were developed by mental health professionals to achieve calmness. Some of these, such as progressive relaxation, are generally referred to as relaxation techniques, while others fall under the broad categories of self-hypnosis, visual imagery, prayer, and meditation. All of these methods promote relaxation and a sense of inner peace. Although the names and terminology are different, they are based on the same principles and physiology.

The Seven Principles of Relaxation

There are elements common to most forms of prayer, meditation, relaxation exercises, and hypnosis. They are:

1. **Breathing rhythmically.** Deep, deliberate, and focused breathing allows you to slow your heartbeat and to center your attention on relaxation. You learned how to do abdominal breathing in the previous chapter.

2. **Focused attention.** Much of anxiety is about nervous anticipation of the future. When you gently focus your attention on the here and now, you transform your experiences into rich and calm experiences. Gentle focused attention activates your frontal lobes to exert their ability to inhibit the overreactivity of your amygdala. Some practices include a "point focus." Focusing on your breathing or on a word, such as a mantra, while meditating can help you stay focused in the present.

3. **A quiet environment.** A quiet environment gives you the opportunity to learn relaxation without distractions. Later, when you are unable to practice in a quiet environment, you can relate back to the way you felt in the quiet place to help you stay focused.

4. **An accepting and nonjudgmental attitude.** By shifting away from rigid expectations and to an accepting attitude, you'll appreciate reality as it is, rather than what you fear it could be. In other words, by not "trying too hard" to relax, you take the pressure off yourself and can relax. Consequently, you'll free yourself to adjust to whatever happens. When you let yourself experience the here and now, instead of fearing the future, you'll be more relaxed and present.

5. **A relaxed posture.** This can include sitting in a relaxed posture or stretching, as you would when practicing yoga (see page 90).

6. **Observation.** By quietly observing each experience, you detach from the compulsion to immediately react to it. Observation allows you to detach from anxiety, by seeing your experiences "from a distance," as if you were not directly affected by them. When you observe your experiences in a nonjudgmental fashion, you simply note what is occurring at the time. Taking the vantage point of an observer, instead of a victim, allows you to detach from the anxiety.

7. **Labeling.** Labeling what you experience accesses your left frontal lobe and its positive emotions. This works if you remain in an accepting and nonjudgmental attitude as a detached observer.

These common principles can lower your anxiety by helping you "let go" of sympathetic nervous system arousal. Shifting your attention to accept and observe the present moment, while simultaneously breathing deeply, promotes relaxation. As a consequence, situations you once associated with anxiety can be experienced with a relaxed attitude. Each principle by itself can help defuse anxiety. When combined, they are particularly powerful in putting you at ease.

LEARNING TO LET GO

Remember that trying too hard to relax actually makes you more tense. Letting go of sympathetic arousal by widening your attention to observe and accept each experience engages your body's ability (through the parasympathetic nervous system) to calm down. By *allowing* yourself to relax, instead of *trying* to relax, you reduce tension so that you *can* relax.

Here's an example. Try not to think of purple elephants. By forcing yourself to keep purple elephants out of your mind, you fight with yourself and invariably think of purple elephants. Now, focus on something else, such as yellow kangaroos. Tell yourself that if purple elephants pop into your mind, it's okay. Simply observe and accept that when purple elephants come to mind, you'll let them in and then just let them go. As you shift your attention to yellow kangaroos, you probably won't think about purple elephants as much, because you let go of the effort to keep purple elephants out of your mind.

Similarly, when you try too hard to keep from being anxious, you make yourself more tense. By focusing on cultivating relaxation skills, instead of trying hard to relax, your anxiety can melt away, because you have widened your focused attention to include acceptance, observance, and a nonjudgmental attitude.

Progressive Relaxation

Progressive relaxation is a popular traditional relaxation technique. It involves tensing and releasing muscle groups, such as your fingers or toes, while simultaneously breathing deeply. Although the seven common principles are traditionally not part of this exercise, I recommend that you include them. When you practice, try not to tense too hard; you want to feel the tension, not give yourself a cramp. Perform the exercise slowly. Don't rush through it as if it were an aerobic exercise.

1. Lie down in a comfortable position. Splay your toes and tense the muscles in your feet. Count to ten, then release the muscles. Notice and enjoy the flow of relaxation for at least 20 seconds. Repeat the tensing, holding, and releasing three times.

2. Splay your fingers and hold for 10 seconds. Release your muscles and, for 20 seconds, notice the relaxing feelings. Repeat this sequence three times.

3. Repeat this progressive relaxation technique for each body part—your calf muscles, forearms, thighs, upper arms, upper legs, pelvic area, stomach muscles, chest muscles, shoulders, neck, and your entire face and scalp—until your entire body is relaxed.

4. Once you have completed the exercise, breathe easily and notice how the muscles in your body feel limp and relaxed. Imagine them being twice as heavy and that your mind is light as air. Think of the relaxation at the end of the exercise as an extended period, so that the calm feelings carry into the next hour.

Although this method is a useful technique for dissipating daytime anxiety, it is not effective for combating insomnia, because the tensing portion of the technique does not dissipate enough for sleep.

However, you can modify the exercise by forgoing the tensing portion and instead repeating the following phrases as you focus on each body part.

> *My feet feel warm and heavy . . .*
> *My ankles feel warm and relaxed . . .*
> *My hips feel relaxed and heavy . . .*
> *My abdomen feels warm and relaxed . . .*
> *My chest feels relaxed . . .*
> *My neck feels comfortable and relaxed . . .*
> *My hands feel heavy and warm . . .*
> *My arms feels warm and relaxed . . .*
> *My forehead feels smooth and relaxed . . .*
> *My jaw feels relaxed and comfortable . . .*
> *My whole body feels heavy, relaxed, and comfortable . . .*

USING IMAGERY TO ACHIEVE A SENSE OF PEACE

Your imagination is a powerful tool, and it can be used to heal your anxiety. You use your imagination every day for periodic daydreaming, so you might as well make it work *for* you, instead of against you. Don't forget that, in your daydreams, you're the main actor as well as the scriptwriter. This means that you can change the storyline to fit your goal of achieving relaxation.

Just as you can imagine the worst, you can also imagine positive experiences. For this reason, imagery is a relaxation technique that has gained popularity in the past thirty years. The therapeutic practice of imagery involves visualizing being in a tranquil place that gives you a sense of peace.

Imagery Exercise

Find a quiet environment and get comfortable. Close your eyes and slow your breathing. Now imagine that relaxing environment and sooth yourself with the imagery. Below is a calming scenario to get you started. Later, you can create any calming scenario you like.

Imagine yourself walking on a secluded beach. The sun is warm on your skin, and there is a gentle sea breeze. You can smell the tang of the sea air. Watch the waves roll in, one after the other, and notice the deep blue color of the sea out beyond the surf. Stop and examine a tide pool; study the pebbly arms of a starfish and the waving fronds of the sea anemones. Embrace all of the visual, auditory, and tactile sensations of the experience: the mist, the crash of the waves, the texture of the sand under your feet. Hear the sound of the surf as it ebbs and flows; make it match every inhalation and exhalation of your breath. Concentrate on a flock of pelicans flying by in formation and taking your anxiety with it. Here are some other scenarios you can use to relax.

The mountain meadow.
Imagine yourself in a mountain meadow in the fall. Smell the aroma of the pines and feel the coolness of the gentle mountain breeze. The leaves of the aspens clatter, and, as you gaze over to them, you notice that they are turning gold in the crisp autumn air. The sight of a mountain peak on the horizon invites your fascination.

Floating on a river.   Imagine yourself on a raft floating down a river. You don't feel like paddling in any particular direction; instead, you let the easy current take you down river. The trees along the river invite your attention. Three deer graze below the canopy of a huge oak.

Imagery can take you away from the anxiety of the day. If you fully absorb yourself in the calming imaginary scenes, you can soothe and refresh yourself. You will feel calm as well as revitalized. Imagery can be used in any meditative or self-hypnotic exercise. Think of transforming your everyday daydreaming into an exercise in engendering a calming feeling of peace and relaxation.

Beth Uses Imagery to Calm Herself

Beth, a graduate student in English literature, came to my anxiety class after a series of panic attacks. She tried using imagery to calm herself down, visualizing herself on a deserted beach. But, before long, she began to hyperventilate and imagined herself running ahead of some villain she couldn't see. When I asked her to interrupt the hyperventilation by using abdominal breathing, the image of running down the beach faded.

Beth tried again and once again imagined herself walking on the beach. Although the panic and the running were gone, she still felt some free-floating anxiety. For Beth, the idea of walking alone on the beach was not soothing. I asked her to imagine a few couples sitting quietly nearby, about fifty yards (forty-five meters) apart. The presence of other people seemed to calm her. I suggested she try the imagery exercise again later using the deserted beach scene, so that she could work on her anxiety about being alone in an exposure exercise (see chapter 8).

The couples anchored in two different spots on the beach gave Beth a sense of security. This initial image helped establish a soothing image. Next, I asked her to incorporate into the exercise the seven principles of relaxation. She had the breathing principle down, and, once she included the other six principles, the beach scene became not only a useful place to "go" when she wanted a "brief vacation" but also a place to practice the seven principles, so she could use them in her daily life. Soon, just reminding herself of the beach scene helped her put the seven relaxation principles into play and feel more at ease.

SELF-HYPNOSIS

Hypnosis is a form of relaxation that uses breathing, imagery, focused attention, and increased receptivity to suggestion and direction, led by one trained in hypnotherapy. *Self*-hypnosis is a method of relaxation and absorption that you induce in yourself. It is easier to do than you might assume.

You might be familiar with "highway hypnosis." Like many people, you probably have driven down the highway, lost in thought. Suddenly, you wonder, "Where did the last ten miles go?" Somehow, you managed to drive that distance on autopilot. Highway hypnosis is an example of how focused attention can take you away from your immediate environment. Although I am not suggesting that you become accomplished at highway hypnosis, it illustrates how easily you can get into a trance state of mind and put your power of concentration to work for you. First, however, you have to dispel the myths that have developed about hypnosis.

> **Myth:** Hypnotic subjects are under the hypnotist's control.
> **Truth:** You are actually in control. That's what self-hypnosis is all about.

Myth: The same techniques are used for all people.

Truth: You can use whatever works for you.

Myth: A person in a hypnotic trance will be unconscious and not remember anything.

Truth: You will remember what you want to remember.

Myth: You can't get out of the trance without a ritual.

Truth: It's easy to shift your attention out of a trance.

When practicing self-hypnosis, it is particularly important to remind yourself that you can "step out of the way," so that your body can relax itself. If you allow your body to do what is natural, the process of self-hypnotic relaxation can unfold naturally.

Self-Hypnosis Exercise

A simple self-hypnotic experience that I teach uses focused breathing and counting down from 10 to 1.

As the numbers decrease, imagine the parts of your body relaxing with each exhalation. Try the following steps, using any of the phrases that fit for you.

10. . . *I am allowing the tension to leave my body with every exhalation.*

9 . . . *I am feeling my body becoming heavy.*

8 . . . *Sounds, physical sensations, and worried thoughts are occurring around my external self, not deep within myself.*

7 . . . *I am descending deeper within myself, as if I am going down an escalator.*

6 . . . *I don't need to fight the relaxation. I can visualize myself drifting with the current down the river. I won't swim upstream, where anxiety lies.*

5 . . . *I am falling deep within myself and gently swaying back and forth, like a feather that drifts to the ground without tension.*

4 . . . *I am deep within myself without worry.*

3 . . . *I am letting go of the old world of anxiety.*

2 . . . *Relaxation and I are one.*

1 . . . *I am at peace with myself in the present moment.*

Now introduce calming posthypnotic suggestions:

I'm learning to put anxiety behind me.
I no longer need to put myself on hyperalert.
There's a calmer part of me that is expanding.
Being calm and focused will be my natural state.

MEDITATION AND PRAYER

Most religions have literature, including manuals, on meditation and prayer. Within Hinduism, Buddhism, Sufism, Judaism, and Christianity, meditation and prayer have a long tradition and have been practiced for thousands of years. The practitioners generally had pious intentions, and the psychological benefits were not well known until the twentieth century, when the positive effects of meditation and prayer were thoroughly researched and found to have a wide range of health benefits, including anxiety reduction. For example, experienced meditators were found to be talented at lowering their blood pressure and slowing down their brain waves. Today, meditation is taught in many medical centers, including my own.

Most types of meditation involve allowing your mind to clear while focusing on your breathing. Clearing your mind occurs by concentrating on a few words, referred to as a mantra, such as Sat Nam. For example, you repeat the word "Sat" on the inhalations and the word "Nam" on the exhalations. By concentrating on the mantra and on your breath, your mind clears and your body relaxes.

Meditation and prayer are embraced by most religious traditions, which suggests that shifting your attention beyond personal concerns, in an attempt to lose a sense of self-identifying awareness and appreciate a wider consciousness, holds great value. The effort to move beyond the personal to the transpersonal is consistent with a theology that conceptualizes our existence as only a small part of the totality of existence. In meditation, when you sense the "wider reality"—that you are but a small part of a greater whole—you detach from the day-to-day attention to your worries. Prayer, when practiced not to achieve some reward, but to simply be closer to God, promotes a deep sense of inner peace. Many methods of praying involve repeating a phrase or entire verses, such as the Lord's Prayer. Like mantras, these phrases serve to direct your attention away from your worries and tension.

If you belong to a church, temple, or mosque, go often to engage in prayer for the purpose of relaxation and the peaceful feelings that you get from the experience. Or you can practice prayer anywhere you choose. Use the seven relaxation principles and give yourself the time to enjoy the anxiety reduction.

All these relaxation exercises require that you set aside some time for regular practice. It can be useful to structure it into your day. Use the following worksheet to monitor your daily efforts and feelings before and after you practice. This will draw attention to how often you practice relaxation exercises and motivate you to practice more often.

RELAXATION MONITORING WORKSHEET

FORM OF RELAXATION	DAY OF THE WEEK	LENGTH OF TIME	MY FEELINGS BEFORE	MY FEELINGS AFTER

Joel Learns Mindfulness Meditation

Joel complained about constant stress at work and had been suffering from GAD, with free-floating anxiety, tension, insomnia, and constant worries. To deal with his anxiety, Joel thought he would try meditation. He was referred to my anxiety class after telling his therapist that he "couldn't seem to get the hang of it."

When asked to describe his method of meditation, he said, "I sit down in that lotus position, and, at first, all I can think about is how my legs ache. Then my mind goes a mile a minute. The more I try to slow it down, the harder it gets."

Joel had a tendency toward trying to maintain control over every aspect of his life, which contributed to his GAD and his lack of success with meditation. The long-term goal was to help him let go of that compulsion.

With Joel in mind, I led the class in an overview of the seven principles of relaxation. As we practiced them, I noticed that Joel tended to breathe shallowly. This was the first bad habit that needed to be changed. Once he learned to breathe abdominally, I suggested that he forget about using the lotus position to meditate and instead sit in a comfortable chair. He responded by saying, "But the people I've seen meditating in books sit in the lotus position!" I suggested that he go with what works, not with what he assumed to be the "correct" method.

I encouraged him to simply observe his experience while meditating and shift to an accepting and non-judgmental attitude about any nuance or experience he encountered, a technique referred to as mindfulness meditation. For example, rather than say, "My neck hurts," he was to simply note that he was experiencing pain in his neck. When he tried this, he discovered that the pain in his neck faded away. When he felt some free-floating anxiety and worries nagged him like a pesky housefly, he didn't try to suppress them, but instead labeled them: "Oh, there's a few worries and some anxiety." Once he labeled his observations, the intensity of his anxiety and the repetition of those worries drifted away.

Joel's meditation style transitioned from using a mantra to using mindfulness meditation.

Mindfulness Meditation

Mindfulness meditation, a type of meditation derived from Buddhism and also referred to as Vipassana or insight meditation, has been widely used in the treatment of anxiety. This technique does not utilize a mantra or praying phrases. Instead, the focus is on breathing, observing, accepting, and employing a nonjudgmental attitude.

When you practice mindfulness meditation, you observe and accept the thoughts, physical sensations, and emotions as they come in and out of your consciousness. You maintain a nonjudgmental attitude as you take a step back from your thoughts, physical sensations, and feelings, seeing them rise and fall back.

Mindfulness meditation has been used in the treatment of general medical problems, such as chronic pain. Instead of trying to block the pain, chronic pain sufferers learn to observe and accept the pain. This concept may seem strange, especially when considering pain. Why accept the pain? Doesn't it bring on more pain? The short answer is no. Actually, you'll have less pain. Mindfulness training can alter how your brain functions and lower your reactivity to pain, because you're not trying to fight it. By observing and accepting the pain, you detach from its intensity.

Overall mindfulness practice has been shown to alleviate stress and cultivate positive feelings, such as the reduction of anxiety. One of the key ways to lower anxiety is through the connections between your prefrontal cortex and your amygdala. These connections play a significant role in your resilience and the ability to maintain positive emotions in the face of adversity.

Your Mindful Brain

The areas of your brain that can defuse anxiety and tame your amygdala are the same areas that are activated during mindfulness meditation. One of these areas is your middle prefrontal cortex, which provides you with the skill of self-observation and has been described as the center of awareness. Long-term meditators are reported to have increased thicknesses of the middle prefrontal cortex as well as an enlarged right insula. The right insula is an area of the cortex that monitors your body functions and, accordingly, how your body feels emotion. The middle prefrontal cortex and the right insula are the areas associated with empathy and self-awareness. The increased thickness of the middle prefrontal cortex is correlated with years of practice and reflects the neuroplasticity that occurred to strengthen this area, so that it works more efficiently.

When you narrate your experience, there is a shift in activation to the left prefrontal cortex. Because your left prefrontal cortex is action-oriented, this activation allows you to put a positive spin on your experiences. When you activate your left hemisphere, there is a greater emphasis on approaching life and facing anxiety, rather than avoiding it, which occurs when you activate your withdrawal-oriented right hemisphere.

Mindfulness involves the use of words, such as "this is a little anxiety," to label your emotional states. Labeling your emotions activates your frontal lobes, especially your left frontal lobe, and reins in the overreactivity of your amygdala.

HYBRID YOGA

In India, yoga has been practiced to promote health and a sense of inner peace for a few thousand years. There are many different types of yoga. The most common is called Hatha Yoga. It is a method of stretching and meditation that can help you deal with anxiety. Hatha Yoga uses a series of poses, in combination with meditation and deep breathing.

More than thirty-five years ago, I stayed briefly in some yoga ashrams in various parts of the world and learned how the poses and meditation worked together. Since then, I have paid close attention to the forty years of research with accomplished yogis that has shown the benefits of yogic techniques. These techniques lead to calming and control over a number of body functions, such as slowing the heart rate down and slowing brain waves as measured by EEG. Small wonder that yoga is taught not only in health clubs and community centers but in medical centers, as well.

Although this book cannot serve as a tutorial on yoga—you can find many fine manuals and classes that serve that purpose—there are some common principles that you can put into practice right now. For example, many traditional yoga postures are essentially stretches, which means you can use your own or those you learned in the previous chapter. Combine the stretches with the breathing and meditative exercises to create a hybrid yoga. Practice your hybrid yoga or traditional yoga to calm yourself.

Carol Finds the Time to Relax

Carol initially came to the class to get help in dealing with panic attacks. After using the anxiety-reduction techniques detailed in this book, her panic attacks faded away. She began with progressive relaxation, then moved to self-hypnosis and meditation with a mantra. Each of these three methods provided a good part of the foundation on which she could build a versatile form of relaxation.

As an elementary school teacher and the mother of two preteens, Carol led a very busy life. In fact, when she first came to the class, she wasn't sure if she had the time to attend regularly. Fortunately, she did commit to scheduling in the time and attended ten sessions. At the eleventh session, she said she wanted to learn how to incorporate what she'd learned about relaxation into her busy schedule.

Carol liked all the relaxation techniques but knew that the demands on her time were so great that, although scheduling in relaxation sounded like a good idea, in practice, she would never get around to it. Coming to the class was different, because there was a social expectation to attend. But structuring in relaxation time at home was much more difficult. There was always something to attend to, a paper to grade or dinner to cook.

She began to incorporate many of the seven principles into her daily life by adopting a mindfulness practice. Even while grading papers, she worked to be completely present, breathing deeply, practicing hybrid yoga.

She returned two months later to report to the class that her regular practices of "Mindful Living," as she put it, had made her life richer and more enjoyable. "It is hard to believe that I was a person plagued by panic attacks and constant anxiety."

Like Carol, you may say to yourself, "I don't have time to do all this!" But not all relaxation exercises require a lot of time. You only need a few moments to slow down your breathing and drop your shoulders. You can remind yourself throughout the day to take a few moments to relax by placing a blue dot on your wristwatch or computer. When you see the dot, stop for five seconds to collect yourself, breath deeply, and meditate. Alternatively, you can identify certain objects as cues to relax. A doorknob or a desk drawer can serve as a reminder to take just a few moments and relax.

Regardless of the type of relaxation technique that appeals to you, regard relaxation as an important skill to cultivate to perfection. Begin to structure relaxation into your day, and pick a particular time to practice—ten to forty minutes before or after going to work or school, for example. Making time for relaxation anoints it as an activity that's as important as sitting down to dinner. You can make it a ritual in which you do certain things to prepare for it. These preparations can resonate with a deep sense of calmness. For example, sit on your bed and meditate for ten minutes before stepping into the shower. However you practice relaxation, it is an important antidote to anxiety. It activates your parasympathetic nervous system to help you calm down and enjoy healing your anxiety.

Every day, do something to cultivate the skills made possible by your sympathetic nervous system. Use any or all of the techniques that you learned in this chapter. Remember that repetition leads to developing habits, and these techniques lead to good habits. Therefore, you should perform more than one relaxation exercise per day. Use the following worksheet to monitor your daily efforts. This exercise helps drive home the importance of relaxation and structuring it into your daily routine. (See page 65 for the worksheet.)

DAILY RELAXATION WORKSHEET

Sunday						
Monday						
Tuesday						
Wednesday						
Thursday						
Friday						
Saturday						
Sunday						
Monday						
Tuesday						
Wednesday						
Thursday						
Friday						
Saturday						
Sunday						
Monday						
Tuesday						
Wednesday						
Thursday						
Friday						
Saturday						
Sunday						
Monday						
Tuesday						
Wednesday						
Thursday						
Friday						
Saturday						

Chapter 7
Change Your Thinking to Change the Way You Feel

Tammy always considered herself an intuitive person. At thirty-two, she had managed to develop a good income as a ceramic artist. Her art reflected what she called "feeling states." All was going well until the economy went south and people had less extra income to buy art. She started to feel anxious about her future. Going with her feelings seemed to work fine, until she had something to feel anxious about.

She told a fellow artist, "My gut tells me that things aren't going to get any better." That friend told her that she had found a way to sell art, despite the downturn in the economy, and invited Tammy to join her. Tammy responded by saying, "It doesn't feel right." Soon, Tammy began to have panic attacks. Between the attacks, she felt a constant current of tension and anxiety. She started to feel that she would soon be experiencing more tragedy, not just a flattened income.

Over the next few months, her friend sold her work through a new retailer; Tammy continued to try to sell hers in the old way, but she couldn't pay the bills. Overwhelmed with anxiety, she finally gave up.

Tammy's situation is extreme, but it illustrates that, although sayings such as "go with your feelings" and "trust your instincts" can work for someone who is *not* plagued by anxiety, when you *do* struggle with anxiety, following these pop-psychology credos does not work. Trusting your feelings without making sure that your mind is participating won't help ease your anxiety. Your mind and your feelings need to work together. Otherwise, your feelings will not be grounded in reality.

Your anxious feelings and thoughts have become bad habits that need to change. In fact, bad thinking habits can create and perpetuate anxious feelings. These are called *thinking errors.* A thinking error can be as simple as the assumption that no one can be trusted. Or it can be more complex, such as believing that you are a psychologically damaged individual who will always suffer from anxiety because of a deeply wounded psyche. In this chapter, you'll learn how to change the way you *think,* so that you can change the way you *feel.* I am asking you to change the way you think before changing the way you feel because you can change your thoughts more easily than you can change your feelings. When you alter your thinking, your feelings will eventually change, too.

Diane Changes Her Thinking
Diane, a computer engineer, was increasingly worried about the longevity of her job after the dot-com bust. Always worried that she would be laid off, she developed a heightened alert system that a layoff might soon happen. Trapped by her own thinking errors, she developed anxiety. It was only after she changed her thinking habits that her anxiety became manageable.

Diane prided herself on being a pessimist. She told friends that if she expected the worst, she would never be disappointed. At work, she would often start a conversation by saying, "Oh, I don't think this new project is going to work out," or "It looks like it's going to be impossible to work out all the bugs in the program."

When situations did get tough, Diane was the one who felt the most stress. Her peers seemed to take it all in stride, yet she felt on edge all the time. Over time, as she braced herself for the next challenge or problem, she began to have trouble sleeping and worried constantly.

She had seen commercials on TV advertising medications for chemical imbalances related to anxiety and depression. Because her coworkers appeared to be untroubled by stress, Diane began to believe she had a chemical imbalance. Although she considered asking her doctor for medications, she kept putting off making an appointment because she worried about missing work.

When the company was bought out, her peers continued to do fine in the face of what Diane thought was great stress. She would walk into a staff meeting, look around, and see that everyone seemed relaxed. She, in contrast, grew to dread staff meetings, often saying on the way in, "Well let's see what management throws at us now. They want us to fail."

Soon Diane began to have panic attacks during the meetings. She would excuse herself and rush to the bathroom. The panic attacks convinced her that something was seriously wrong with her. One day, her panic attack was so acute that she went to the emergency room, convinced that her shortness of breath was evidence of a heart attack. After his examination, the emergency room physician told her that her heart was fine and that, in fact, she had had a panic attack. He then referred her to me. During our first appointment, I worked with Diane on the techniques you learned in the preceding chapters, such as abdominal breathing and mindfulness. It quickly became clear that she suffered from thinking errors and negative self-talk, which impeded the rest of her treatment. We needed to deal with those thinking errors right away.

We explored her automatic thoughts, assumptions, and core beliefs (which you'll learn about later in the chapter) and discovered that she harbored a deep-seated pessimism; she expected the worst and actually set herself up to experience the worst. For example, if she and her fellow employees received a bonus check, she assumed that management would soon demand that they work overtime without pay to recover the money from the bonus check. It became evident that she constructed her beliefs with such rigidity and negativity that they offered her no option but to feel anxious in response to new experiences, including new assignments at work. Although she wanted to be positively surprised by these new experiences, she painted herself into a psychological corner by viewing new situations in a narrow and negative context, so that she wouldn't be disappointed.

In our sessions, Diane learned to shift away from her pessimistic outlook and construct a series of assumptions that helped her react to events with greater adaptability than she ever thought possible. Her new thinking skills allowed her not only to adapt to the changes at work but also to consider those changes as opportunities for a healthy challenge. Had we not dealt with her bad thinking habits, we could not have moved on to the next level of treatment. She learned to prevent panic attacks and deal with stress much more effectively.

YOUR THINKING INFLUENCES YOUR FEELINGS

Like Diane, the way you *think* about new experiences has much to do with how you're going to *feel* about them. And like her, you can reframe the way you think to change the way you feel about the situations you encounter. I'm not suggesting that you simply put a happy face on things. That is, of course, too superficial. I'm asking you to actually rewire your brain. As you learned in chapter 3, the more you repeat an action or think in a particular way, the more likely you are to turn these actions and thoughts into habits. These habits develop at the synaptic level through neuroplasticity, the process of making new connections between your neurons. In this chapter, you'll learn how to get the frontal lobes of your brain to rein in your amygdala.

When you're plagued by anxiety, your amygdala—the part of your brain deep in your temporal lobes that is generally hyperactive in people with anxiety disorders—gets its way. Your amygdala hijacks your frontal lobes, which function to direct your attention, and get the better of your capacity for reason. Your job is to help your left frontal lobe get activated, so that you can regain control over your experiences. You can tame your amygdala by training your frontal lobes "to decide" what not to be fearful of. By reality testing—basing your beliefs on what is real and not on what you feel—you can control your fear center. In other words, you decide whether a threat really exists by basing your decision on the facts of a particular situation, rather than on your feelings alone.

Dan Bases a Threat on His Feelings

Dan came to my anxiety class after his wife Joanna told him that she was at her "wits' end" with him. Apparently, the campground they usually stayed at for their summer vacation was closed. They were issued a new permit for a campground a few miles away. Dan said that he wanted to cancel the vacation because he didn't know about the security at the new campground. His wife complained that he had no evidence that the security in the new campground was questionable. He countered that they had no evidence that it was good. "Besides," he said, "the whole change doesn't feel right."

If you're like most people who suffer from anxiety, you underactivate your left frontal lobe, which is associated with positive feelings and action, and overactivate your right frontal lobe, which is associated with negative feelings and withdrawal. The language skills of your left frontal lobe make the effectiveness of cognitive behavioral therapy (CBT) possible. CBT addresses the cognitive distortions and thinking errors that underlie anxiety. Through cognitive restructuring—changing the way you think—you activate your left frontal lobe and confront the cognitive distortions and thinking errors.

By cognitive restructuring, you confront the rigidity and boxed-in negativity head-on. You employ your underutilized left frontal lobe through taking action, verbal labeling, and reality testing. In other words, when you encounter a potential anxiety-provoking situation, you describe in realistic terms the challenge you face and then take action to meet the challenge. Because your left frontal lobe is capable of working with specific, bite-size details, it balances your right frontal lobe's tendency to be "big picture–oriented" and overwhelmed by anxiety.

Tim Practices Verbal Labeling

Tim, a thirty-five-year-old librarian, had increasingly developed anxiety when in the presence of strangers. He hated it when his supervisor assigned him to the checkout desk, because he knew that he was expected to make small talk with patrons as they checked out books, and just the thought of it filled him with anxiety.

After a few weeks in my anxiety class, Tim began to practice verbal labeling techniques. We agreed that he would identify and label a detail related to the book that a patron checked out. In this way, he could move away from feeling overwhelmed and shift to the detail-oriented and positive feelings of his left hemisphere.

As a patron came up to check out a book, Tim said, "Oh, *Cold Mountain*! That book has been one of our most popular ones for years. You'll enjoy it." "Thanks," said the patron. "I'll look forward to reading it even more now." Tim managed to label a positive emotion by using the word *enjoy*, even though it was about reading a book, and make small talk at the same time. He proved to himself that he could pay attention to a positive detail outside of his feelings of anxiety and enjoy interactions with others.

When you relabel an experience, your left frontal lobe contributes its tendency toward positive feelings and its can-do attitude. Also, the "approach tendency" of your left frontal lobe works to counterbalance the withdrawal tendency of the right frontal lobe, especially during the critical exposure challenge, which I'll describe in the next chapter. Take a few minutes to determine whether you are mislabeling your experiences. Although the following list may seem rather obvious to you, you might be surprised by the number of statements you think are true. Do you have any of the following mistaken beliefs? Circle "T" for true or "F" for false.

COMMON MISTAKEN BELIEFS

I have trouble with stress.	T	F
I should always be competent.	T	F
It is unwise to trust people	T	F
Worrying about a problem lessens the severity.	T	F
Failing is horrible.	T	F
Sometimes it's hard to be alone.	T	F
I am embarrassed about my anxiety condition.	T	F
Life is often a struggle.	T	F
There is something fundamentally wrong with me.	T	F
When someone criticizes me, I am devastated.	T	F
My anxiety condition is hopeless.	T	F
I demand perfection from myself.	T	F
I can't control my emotions.	T	F
I'm beyond help.	T	F
My brain is defective.	T	F
The damage is done and there's no going back.	T	F
Why set goals if I never achieve them?	T	F
My feelings tell me what to believe.	T	F

UNUSUAL MISTAKEN BELIEFS

If I look into people's eyes, they'll know I'm nervous.	T	F
If my hair looks bad, it'll be a bad day.	T	F
A deep trauma occurred in my life.	T	F
Someone will find out that I'm incompetent.	T	F
Once people get to know me, they don't like me.	T	F
Life wears down my ability to cope.	T	F
I go from crisis to crisis.	T	F
My father made me feel nervous all the time.	T	F
One of these days, I'm going to lose it.	T	F
Some day, people will find out that I'm mentally ill.	T	F

Many people in my anxiety classes tend to answer true to several of the previous statements. If you answered true to any of them, you are setting yourself up to feel more anxious and less in control of anxiety. This is because you box yourself in with expectations that give you little flexibility and room to be human. You need to restructure your beliefs, so that you have a fighting chance to manage your anxiety.

RESTRUCTURING YOUR BELIEFS

You are the narrator of your own life. The tone and perspective with which you describe each experience generates feelings associated with that narration. For example, if you find yourself constantly assuming, "This is hard," "I wonder whether I'm going to survive," or "It looks like this is going to turn out badly," you'll generate anxious feelings. It's time to restructure the way you think. Underlying this narration are the beliefs that frame your experience and give it meaning. Think of your beliefs as having many layers.

On the surface are your *automatic thoughts*. These are like short tapes that momentarily flash through your mind. Call these automatic thoughts a form of "self-talk" that you use as you navigate through the day. You produce a wide variety of these automatic thoughts, some consciously and some unconsciously. For example, automatic thoughts that fuel anxiety go something like this: You walk into a room, see a few new people, and say to yourself, "Oh no, I don't like this. This is not good." Or, "These people will soon find out that I am full of anxiety and will reject me." Automatic thoughts are bad habits that cloud fresh and positive experiences. They can turn a potentially good experience into one fraught with anxiety. If you tell yourself that you are always stressed or full of anxiety before doing something new, that new experience will be tainted by that anxiety.

Automatic thoughts that cultivate anxiety include:

Either/or thinking.   Simply put, either you feel anxious or you feel calm, and you believe there are no feelings in between. You constrain yourself into rigid thinking and have trouble thinking beyond black-or-white, either/or, and right-or-wrong possibilities. If you suffer from either/or thinking, develop the ability to see the shades of gray. When you see new people, instead of telling yourself that the situation is terrible, learn to get comfortable with these unfamiliar people. For example, Josh, a museum tour guide, learned that it was natural to feel a little anxiety when meeting the new people on his tours. The anxiety helped him stay on his toes and explain things when museum visitors seemed confused. If Josh thought in an either/or way, his minor anxiety would become overwhelming, and he would lose his capacity to be alert. Instead, he acknowledged a little anxiety as normal, which helped him defuse the potential to be overwhelmed with the assumption that a little anxiety is too much anxiety.

Overestimating or exaggerating risk.   If you walk outside and see a few clouds, you automatically assume a major storm is on the way and that your house will be flooded. When you regularly expect disaster, you increase your anxiety. Exaggerating risk is a less extreme, but more common, version of catastrophizing (which you'll read about later in this chapter). For example, the presence of a new person may stir thoughts that he will threaten your safety. On the other hand, the new person is someone you don't yet know anything about, so why jump to conclusions? Barbara faced a challenge when she said goodbye to her old friends next door and new people moved into the house. Not only did she feel the loss of good friends, but she was also now faced with getting to know her neighbors, which made her anxious, because she didn't think she had the social skills to get to know them. It had taken her a few years to get to know her old neighbors, and the friendship developed largely because of their efforts. Barbara eventually decided that the loss of her friends didn't have to be a catastrophe. It became an opportunity to meet new people.

Emotional reasoning. You say to yourself, "I have a gut feeling that something is going to go wrong." The problems with this gut feeling are that it is a false alarm and that you feel it too often. You might regard a particular emotion as evidence of the truth, instead of looking at the facts. An example is thinking, "I feel nervous, so it must mean something bad is going to happen." To challenge this faulty reasoning, you need to look at the facts and tell yourself, "I know I feel anxious, but there is no evidence that there is anything to feel anxious about."

Your feelings need to be overtaken by reality testing. Reality testing simply means that you base your beliefs on what you know to be true—on what you have hard evidence for. Remember Tammy? She suffered from an extreme version of emotional reasoning. She eventually learned to use reason and make better business decisions, so that she could let her art reflect her feelings.

You probably have a variety of your own automatic thoughts. Use this worksheet to write down the negative automatic thoughts that fuel your anxiety, then refute them with corrective automatic thoughts. Make sure the corrective automatic thoughts include flexibility and promote adaptability. Copy this list and carry it with you, so that you can refer to it often. Practice these often, so that they become new habits.

WHAT ARE YOUR AUTOMATIC THOUGHTS?

OLD AUTOMATIC THOUGHTS	CORRECTIVE AUTOMATIC THOUGHTS

You can develop automatic thoughts that will serve you much better than those that trigger anxiety. These are some that can help you turn a stressful experience into a positive one:

- This problem or challenge is an opportunity.
- I can do this.
- I can cope with how things turn out.
- Things will look up soon.
- I'll do the best that I can.
- This will be a valuable learning experience.
- I can appreciate the shades of gray.
- I'll use my mind to judge the situation, not my feelings.
- I can learn to be more accepting of anxiety.
- Here's an opportunity to meet new people.
- I can adapt to this situation, even if I don't like it.
- This is interesting, even if it is a bit bizarre.
- I can enjoy myself, even when I'm anxious.
- A little anxiety is good—it keeps me alert.
- I'll focus on the positive, despite the negative people.

Take a moment to construct a variety of new automatic thoughts. Practice them on a regular basis, so that your brain can rewire and make them new habits. Practice self-talk using them, so that they become new automatic thoughts. Approach this exercise by developing automatic thoughts that are positive, hopeful, optimistic, and adaptive.

New Automatic Thoughts

_____   _____

_____   _____

_____   _____

_____   _____

_____   _____

_____   _____

_____   _____

_____   _____

_____   _____

Overgeneralizing. You hear on the morning radio traffic report that a there is a backup on a particular highway, so you assume that all the roads are jammed. This thinking error occurs when you use small pieces of information or details to paint a broad, entirely negative picture. This is worse than thinking that the glass is half full—it's believing that the glass has nothing in it at all.

Kathleen fell into this thinking trap. Always called a "drama queen" by some of her friends at college, she had a tendency to label a class a "grade killer" if the professor lectured without using a PowerPoint program. She'd work herself up into such an anxiety state that her grades suffered because she found it hard to concentrate. Meanwhile, her classmates adapted to the unique format of the professor.

You need to replace bad thinking habits with good thinking habits by generating new automatic thoughts to refute and contradict the old negative automatic thoughts. Let's say you feel a panic attack coming on. If you don't change your thinking—and the negative self-talk that goes with those thinking errors—your old automatic thoughts will turn everything into a catastrophic experience.

In the left column that follows, you'll find negative automatic thoughts. In the right column are alternatives you can use to refute those automatic thoughts.

Do any of these negative thoughts sound familiar? Notice how the corrective automatic thoughts give you flexibility to be human and grow. The corrective automatic thoughts bring in reality and hope.

OLD AUTOMATIC THOUGHTS	CORRECTIVE AUTOMATIC THOUGHTS
Oh my God! Here it goes again.	This happened before and I survived.
Something terrible will happen.	But nothing terrible ever happens.
I need to get out of here.	I can stay right where I am.
This will always happen.	Not if I change things.
I need help.	I can and will help myself.
They'll discover that I'm nervous.	If they do, it's no big deal.
He sees right through me.	I have nothing to hide.
They're all relaxed.	Good. And I can be, too!
There are too many people here.	The more to get to know!

CHANGING YOUR ASSUMPTIONS

Your *assumptions* are positioned midway between your automatic thoughts and core beliefs, which I discuss later in the chapter. They are a translator between them. They aren't as fundamental as core beliefs, yet they aren't as superficial as automatic thoughts.

Assumptions are like mini theories about the world, people, and yourself. Self-limiting assumptions are often laced with words such as *should, never, always, must,* and *everyone.* For example, you might say to yourself "I'm *always* nervous around other people." This assumption boxes you into feeling nervous around other people. The assumptions of "I *never* adapt well to change," or "I *always* need to be in control to feel comfortable," set any new situation beyond your comfort level.

Negative assumptions are rigid and inflexible and give you few options to succeed. As a result, you feel tense and anxious. You need to change your assumptions, so they are flexible and reasonable. You need to modify your assumptions, so that they serve you well and are based in reality. They need to be adaptable, to give you the opportunity to cope with changing conditions.

Automatic thoughts are quick snapshots that you use in particular situations; assumptions are theories that you carry with you in many situations. The table at the bottom of the page shows some examples of assumptions and ways to correct them. Some thinking errors invite faulty assumptions, such as the following:

Magical thinking.   "If I worry about this situation enough, the worst won't happen." Magical thinking is like superstition. You make connections where there are no reasonable connections. Magical thinking increases anxiety by making its causes intangible and not based in reality.

Giving up.   "If driving on the freeway makes me nervous, it's best to avoid the freeway." Giving up increases the feeling of being overwhelmed. It is an extreme form of avoidance because you convince yourself that you aren't up to the challenge.

Asking unanswerable questions.   "Will I get laid off next year and lose my house?" "Is my loved one going to get a serious illness when we get older?" Asking questions laced with negativity about the distant future promotes anxiety.

Control obsession.   "I need to be in control." If you have an intense need to maintain a sense of control over the events in your life, you set yourself up for rude awakenings. You are not in total control of all the events in your life, never have been, and never will be. You can have a certain amount of control over some aspects of events, but never total control. The degree of control you may have over any event is based on a realistic assessment of what is truly possible—not what you hope to control. The bottom line is that you can't be in control of everything.

Catastrophizing.   This involves turning situations into the worst-case scenario. For example, during a panic attack, you may say to yourself, "I'm going to have a heart attack and die!" To de-catastrophize, you'll need to talk yourself down by asking yourself questions, such as, "When was the last time I died from one of these panic attacks?" Use helpful statements, such as "Every time I think the worst is going to happen, it doesn't," or "I was good at making mountains out of molehills. Now I am going to let molehills stay molehills."

NEGATIVE ASSUMPTIONS	CORRECTIVE ASSUMPTIONS
I always lose control of my emotions.	But I haven't lost control yet.
I must control my emotions	I'm learning how to control them.
I never seem to handle anxiety well.	I am learning to handle anxiety better.
I should be more competent.	I'm getting more competent.
Everyone feels less nervous than I do.	I really don't know what others feel.

You probably have plenty of your own assumptions. Use this worksheet to write down the negative assumptions that fuel your anxiety, then refute them with corrective assumptions. Make the corrective assumptions not only refute the negative ones but also give you portable mini theories to carry around and help you adjust to changing situations that you encounter every day.

CORRECT YOUR ASSUMPTIONS

NEGATIVE ASSUMPTIONS	CORRECTIVE ASSUMPTIONS

Just as you did with automatic thoughts, you can develop many anxiety-reducing assumptions that will serve you better than those that trigger anxiety. Here are several that can help you turn a stressful experience into a positive one:

- I'm learning new coping skills.
- I'll do the best I can, and that will be good enough.
- I can appreciate the full range of possibilities.
- I'm becoming more confident.
- I'm just as worthy as the next person.
- I don't need to control every detail in my life.

Take a moment to construct your own unique assumptions. Make sure that your new assumptions give you flexibility and do not contain such words as *should, must, never, always,* and *everyone.* You'll be coming back to this list often to help you stay focused on what you need to practice.

Keep this list with you, so you can refer to it often. You can add to and fine-tune it to make it apply to the changing circumstances in your life. Practice these regularly, so that your brain can rewire and develop new habits. By rewiring your brain through repetition, you'll create a new set of healthy assumptions.

NEW ASSUMPTIONS

_____   _____

_____   _____

_____   _____

_____   _____

_____   _____

_____   _____

_____   _____

_____   _____

Tia's New Assumptions

After struggling with feelings of anxiety and periodic panic attacks for ten years, Tia decided she finally needed help. She came to my anxiety class expecting to be told that she was beyond hope. It became evident that she limited herself with many negative assumptions and was convinced that she had bad genes. She assumed that she needed to avoid stress at all costs. But, because she avoided potentially stressful events, what she soon assumed to be too stressful were events and situations that she had managed to cope with in the past.

During the anxiety class, her peers shared their negative assumptions, such as "I'm beyond help now. My problems are unique. What helps others won't help me." She identified with each of them. However, when they told her that they soon got over those negative assumptions and replaced them with positive assumptions, Tia said, "I think I'm too far gone." Almost in a chorus, her fellow class members said, "That's what we thought, too."

With the encouragement of her peers, Tia began to shift from negative assumptions to positive ones. Specifically, she shifted from "I'm beyond help now" to "I'm seeking help." And "My problems are unique" became "I can see that others have had similar problems." And finally, "What helps others won't help me" became "I don't know whether they won't help unless I try." Try she did. Over the next few weeks, she managed to untie herself from the constraints of her negative assumptions and open herself up to the potential for change.

RESTRUCTURING YOUR CORE BELIEFS

Your assumptions can be ways to cope with your core beliefs. Core beliefs are broad generalizations about yourself and how the world works. When the beliefs are associated with anxiety, they paint you into a corner psychologically, so that whatever you do, you're faced with an insurmountable challenge—one that will always fail.

Negative core beliefs can include the assumption that you are a deeply damaged person or that you don't have what it takes to make use of any kind of help. These core beliefs keep you from believing that you can find relief from anxiety. They set you up to fail because you leave yourself no hope. By changing your assumptions, as you did in the worksheet above, you can begin to chip away at your anxiety-producing core beliefs.

Another way of dealing with your core beliefs is to confront them directly. Many of your core beliefs developed as you were growing up. Perhaps your parents taught you that the world was a dangerous place and that you always needed to be on your guard. Or maybe you were led to believe that you were inadequate and incapable of succeeding.

Most likely you developed a much less extreme version of core beliefs, which formed as you either succeeded or failed at projects and major challenges during your life. If you succeeded, you developed feelings of adequacy; if you failed, you might have developed feelings of inadequacy. Perhaps you had some unfortunate social experiences, such as being rejected or ridiculed, or told you were inadequate. Some core beliefs include:

- The world is a dangerous place.
- People can't be trusted.
- Life is a struggle.
- Things always go wrong.
- I'm defective.
- I can't cope.
- I'm inadequate.
- My mother damaged me deeply.
- Something in my childhood traumatized me, but I can't remember it.
- I took too many drugs in my youth, and there's nothing left of my brain.
- God is making me pay for my sins.
- I had a breakdown and there's no pulling it all back together.
- I will always be dysfunctional because I know no other way of being.
- I'm jinxed to have bad luck and anxiety around people.

Core-belief thinking traps can lead to anxiety. They all share a common tendency to "lock in" expectations of how things "ought to be."

Use the worksheet below to identify the core beliefs that fuel your anxiety. Refute these core beliefs in the column on the right.

REFUTE YOUR STRESSFUL CORE BELIEFS

OLD CORE BELIEF	REFUTED CORE BELIEF

Now, take a few moments to identify the core beliefs that you would like to cultivate. In other words, instead of simply refuting core beliefs, construct *new* ones that are fresh and have vitality, strength, adaptability, perseverance, resilience, and optimism. For example, think of yourself as a spiritual and compassionate person. Perhaps you can cultivate a sense of adventure. Your new core beliefs should help you define yourself as a person who is capable, adaptive, and resilient. "I bounce back from adversity. I'm like a duck—water rolls off my back. I can travel the world by myself and meet new people along the way."

Refer to your core-beliefs worksheet often, just as you did with the automatic thoughts and assumptions worksheets. Reflect on how these new core beliefs are fundamental to your self-esteem and to the way you see yourself.

NEW CORE BELIEFS

_____   _____
_____   _____
_____   _____
_____   _____
_____   _____
_____   _____
_____   _____
_____   _____
_____   _____

Here are some common examples:

The Perfectionist   If you think of yourself as a perfectionist, you set yourself up to be disappointed in yourself, because nothing turns out perfectly. Because things don't work out perfectly, you might think that you are inadequate or have failed. By being locked into expecting perfection, you drive yourself into anxiety. Allow yourself to be human, which by definition is to be imperfect.

The Pessimist   By thinking of yourself as a pessimist, you create a self-fulfilling prophesy. You'll expect the worst and feel the anxious emotions associated with the worst. You'll also do little to promote the best because you don't expect that it's possible. You might say to yourself, "Why try? Things always turn out badly."

The Victim   If you feel you are a victim, you will feel victimized by whatever happens, no matter how negative or positive the experience. Ironically, your victim role can make you easy prey to those who are in the habit of taking advantage of people like you. This is because bullies tend to pick on people who are easy to manipulate. You can also develop an identity of being a martyr or a codependent. In this case, you feel that it is your job to take care of those who take advantage of you.

The Critic   Being critical of events or situations is easy in the short term, because it's not hard to find imperfections. But in the long run, it's hard on you because you'll find fault with everything, including yourself. And because nothing in life is without faults, you end up feeling bad. Constant criticism increases your tension and anxiety, because finding fault puts you and those around you on edge.

These and other core beliefs are thinking traps that you can refute by developing counter-beliefs. Consider the following examples of core beliefs. See how you can refute them with beliefs in the column on the right.

OLD CORE BELIEF	REFUTED CORE BELIEF
I should be able to do things perfectly.	I can allow myself to be human.
I expect the worst, for good reason.	There's no reason to expect the worst.
Bad things happen to me.	Both good and bad things happen.
There is always something wrong.	There's often a silver lining.
My future was damaged early in life.	I can write my own future.
Anxiety is who I am.	Anxiety is a bad habit that I'll break.
Anxiety is a family tradition.	It is a tradition that I will leave.
I'm a worrier.	I will learn to worry less.
I'm different from others.	Everyone is different.

It is critical that you develop more effective core beliefs that will serve you much better than those that trigger anxiety. The new core beliefs will form the foundation for your assumptions and automatic thoughts. Once you develop new core beliefs, you'll need to recite them to yourself often so that they become part of you. Here are some that can help you turn a stressful experience into a fresh and positive one:

- I'm a capable person.
- I'm a worthwhile and worthy person.
- I'm flexible and adaptable.
- I don't allow people or situations to victimize me.
- I can find silver linings in situations.
- I can turn an awkward social situation into something enjoyable.
- When people get to know me, they think I'm funny.
- I mean well and try hard, and that is enough.
- I'm an optimist, even around pessimistic people.
- I hunger for personal growth and challenge.

Your job is to restructure your core beliefs, so that you have a fair chance at defusing anxiety.

SETTING GOALS TO BOOST YOUR SELF-ESTEEM

Your self-esteem and self-confidence are connected. Self-esteem describes how you feel about yourself; self-confidence is believing that you are capable of accomplishment. Usually, confidence grows from your past experiences. You can deal with your anxiety by setting goals and accomplishing them to boost your self-confidence and, in turn, your self-esteem. When you accomplish things, you feel better about yourself. This means that you need to *do things,* so that you can feel good about what you do. Take a class, for example, or complete a project, however small. By accomplishing your goals, you will not only feel more confident, but you will also be activating your left frontal lobe, which taps into the positive feelings that it processes.

Be sure to set challenging but achievable goals to help reconstruct your sense of self-esteem in response to anxiety. Break them up into achievable short-term goals that move you toward completing the long-term goal, so you can see the progress you are making.

Working toward completing your goals also activates your left frontal lobe, so you achieve a sense of control over your anxiety and spend increasingly less time feeling overwhelmed by it. As an example, let's say that you want to be less anxious about speaking in front of large groups of people. In the past, just thinking about this made you panic. You'll need to work toward developing self-confidence by seeing yourself speaking successfully in front of people.

Break down the goal as shown:

Long-Term Goal:

Speaking in front of large groups of people.

Short-term goals supporting the long-term goal:

Speaking in front of two people several times.
Speaking in front of four people several times.
Speaking in front of eight people several times.
Speaking in front of sixteen people several times.

_____

_____

Here's another example, for becoming more comfortable about flying.

Long-Term Goal:

Getting over my phobia about flying on airplanes.

Short-term goals supporting the long-term goal:

Seeing fun movies about flying on airplanes.
Going to the airport and watching the planes fly in and out.
Taking a short flight to a neighboring city.
Taking a long flight.

_____

_____

In this chapter, we laid the groundwork for reducing anxiety by changing your automatic thoughts, assumptions, and core beliefs and by setting some constructive goals for yourself. In the next chapter, you'll learn to deal with the symptoms of anxiety by putting them into context.

Use this worksheet to develop your short- and long-term goals. Make sure that they are linked, so that the short-term goals are intermediate steps toward the completion of the long-term goals.

LONG-TERM GOAL	LONG-TERM GOAL

Short-term goals supporting the long-term goal	Short-term goals supporting the long-term goal

LONG-TERM GOAL	LONG-TERM GOAL

Short-term goals supporting the long-term goal	Short-term goals supporting the long-term goal

Chapter 8
Facing Your Fears

When you avoid what you fear, your fear grows. This fact is difficult to grasp, because when you avoid what you fear over the short term, your fear temporarily decreases. Over the long term, however, avoidance allows that anxiety to flourish. Say, for example, that you are anxious about going to a party because you fear talking to strangers. When you avoid the party, your anxiety lessens. But if you avoid the next party invitation and then the next and the next, you now have a problem, because your avoidance has made your anxiety about talking to strangers worse than it was to begin with. Pamela fell into this trap.

Pamela's Avoidance Behaviors

Pamela had been feeling ill at ease since she moved to a new condo complex. She didn't know the neighbors and felt awkward about starting at square one, introducing herself and getting to know them. She thought that because the other condo owners all knew one another, they were on firmer ground when socializing at the complex parties. She would be under a spotlight, singled out as the "new person." So, when Pamela was invited to the parties, she found convenient excuses to bow out. Yet, each time she turned down an invitation, she worried that the other owners would think of her as antisocial. Soon, her anxiety increased to the point where she avoided engaging with them at all. When she saw one of her neighbors in the parking lot, she pretended she didn't see them or that she had forgotten something in her car and ducked her head back in to hide.

Finally, Pamela came in to talk to me about her increasing anxiety. Her discomfort over socializing with others in the complex had become such a problem that she worried constantly about what might happen if she found herself in a situation where she had no choice but to say something, such as when she and a neighbor were standing next to one another.

She was losing sleep and felt tense much of the time. She also suffered from free-floating anxiety. I explained to Pamela that her avoidance had actually become the problem. She responded by saying, "Why not stay away from what is making me anxious? When I feel more at ease, I'll start talking to all of them." I told her that she was in quicksand, and, until she got out, she would just sink deeper. Pamela had to learn to avoid her avoidance and face her fears.

In this chapter, you'll learn to work against avoidance, even though it seems to make you feel better. I call this *challenging the paradox*. Challenging the paradox involves doing away with avoidance and replacing it with *exposure*—facing what makes you feel anxious. By exposing yourself to anxiety-provoking situations, you become habituated to them, and your anxiety will actually diminish over the long term.

Before we discuss the ways to neutralize anxiety by exposure, it will be helpful to determine the degree to which you are engaging in avoidant behaviors. Answer the following questions by circling "Y for yes or "N" for no.

AVOIDANCE QUESTIONNAIRE

DO YOU:	
Try to avoid situations that make you anxious?	Y N
Continually monitor your anxiety level?	Y N
Find increasingly "effective" ways to avoid anxiety?	Y N
Search situations for things that may cause anxiety	Y N
Find that the range of your activities has shrunk?	Y N
Think that any anxiety is bad anxiety?	Y N
Avoid challenges that might be stressful?	Y N
Procrastinate often?	Y N
Avoid social situations that are challenging?	Y N
Abruptly leave a situation if it stirs up anxiety?	Y N
Find ways to distract yourself from anxiety?	Y N
Isolate yourself from people you find intimidating?	Y N
Avoid any form of stress more than you did a year ago?	Y N
Carry around an antianxiety pill, just in case?	Y N
Sit at the back of a room so you can easily escape?	Y N
Offer your opinion only if forced?	Y N
Consider those who don't share your opinions scary?	Y N
Go to the same restaurant because it's familiar?	Y N
Want to go back to when the world was simpler?	Y N

If you answered yes to any of the above questions, you are embracing avoidance over exposure. The greater the number of yes responses you circled, the greater your degree of avoidance and the greater the probability that you are promoting anxiety.

FORMS OF AVOIDANCE

Several types of avoidant behaviors contribute to anxiety. They include *escape, avoidance, procrastination,* and *safety* behaviors.

Escape behaviors are things you do in the heat of the moment when you are in an anxiety-provoking situation. You essentially escape the situation to flee from anxiety. Say, for example, that you are in a room with a crowd of people and you begin to feel anxious. Abruptly fleeing the room is an escape behavior.

Avoidance behaviors are things you do to stay away from anxiety-provoking experiences. Perhaps a friend invites you to meet him at the home of one of his colleagues. Because you don't know your friend's colleague, you decide that going to his home would provoke intolerable anxiety, so you don't go. That's an avoidance behavior.

Procrastination means that you put off things because it's "easier" on your stress level. For example, you put off going to the colleague's home, waiting until the very last moment to finally go. That's procrastination.

Safety behaviors are things that you do or carry with you to distract you or give you a sense of safety. Say you go the colleague's home to meet your friend and begin to feel anxious. To prevent yourself from tumbling into a panic attack, you begin to fiddle with your watchband to draw your focus away from the others. That's a safety behavior.

All of these methods of dealing with anxiety are ways of staying away from anxiety. They are all forms of avoidance, and they keep you from habituating to the situation and learning to overcome the anxiety.

Because avoidant behaviors result in a temporary reduction of fear, they serve as powerful short-term reinforcements. They are, therefore, difficult to resist. Soon your avoidance can become increasingly elaborate. If taken to the extreme, you can become agoraphobic, afraid to leave your home. Once you begin avoiding, it's difficult to stop.

Why is it so easy to use avoidance?

- It reduces fear in the short term.
- There is a superficial logic to avoidance:

"Why wouldn't I avoid something that makes me anxious?"

- You receive some secondary gain from it, such as extra care, because people around you feel sympathy.

Avoiding situations that cause anxiety starts a destructive spiral that works something like this:

The more you engage in avoidant behaviors, the harder it is to resist repeating them in the future, because they become habits.

Even distraction is a mild form of avoidance. When you distract yourself from anxiety-provoking situations, you are not getting the full positive effect of the exposure. Yes, I mean positive! Here's how it works. Learning requires attention, and attention is directed by your frontal lobes. If you focus your attention somewhere other than on the situation in front of you, your frontal lobes do not direct your full resources to habituating yourself to it and making it routine. Shifting your attention away from a situation prevents you from learning how to habituate to the situation.

An obsession with being in control can also lead to avoidance. By trying to control every experience to minimize anxiety, you put yourself into a mode of always trying to anticipate the future, so that you can steer yourself away from the *possibility* of anxiety. Here's where your avoidant behaviors can get rather elaborate. When you anticipate what *might* happen, you brace yourself for anxiety that you might not experience. Anxiety often results from anticipating the worst-case scenario. When you avoid situations, you put yourself at a realistic disadvantage, because you never get to prove to yourself that the worst rarely happens. You put yourself on hyperalert for detecting anxiety-provoking experiences, then perceive even minor events as dangerous.

Trying to control your emotions is a tricky business. Complete control is impossible. Not allowing yourself to experience a moderate degree of emotional flexibility sets you up to constantly brace for an emotion outside your tolerance level. This is especially true if you are rigid about anticipating the future. Take Irene, who strove to minimize "stress" at any level. This meant that she avoided anything requiring the slightest degree of adjustment. Ironically, everything she encountered required some degree of adjustment. The result was that she felt constant anxiety, because she couldn't control her emotions.

You can untie yourself from this trap by shifting to a here-and-now focus. As you learned in chapter 6, when you are mindfully present and focus on accepting what is happening right now, instead of on what *might* occur in the future, you can detach from anxiety.

If you are a skier, you know that leaning back on your skis makes you fall. Inexperienced skiers unknowingly try to slow themselves down or keep themselves from falling by doing exactly the thing that will make them fall—lean back. When you deal with anxiety by avoiding the things you fear, you are essentially leaning back on your skis. In other words, if you embrace the challenge of each experience, instead of fighting it, you will be more successful at conquering your fear of that experience. When you try to stay clear of anxiety by minimizing anything that makes you anxious, anxiety plagues you even more.

How does this work? The more you retreat from an anxiety-provoking situation, the more anxiety-provoking situations your avoidance creates. Soon, you will be vigilant about what *might* be anxiety-provoking. So, you limit yourself to activities and situations that you believe are free of anxiety. When you encounter a little anxiety in a situation that you thought was anxiety-free, you begin to avoid *that* situation in the future. Soon, the range of your activities shrinks. As your world shrinks, the things that trigger anxiety increase. In the extreme, this kind of shrinkage results in agoraphobia. People with agoraphobia avoid the world outside their home because they have grown to fear the outside.

Escape and avoidant behaviors are sneaky and undermining. On the surface, these behaviors seem to make sense. An escape behavior, for example, provides you with an easy way out of an anxiety-provoking experience when things seem too difficult to handle. Because it's hard to resist, you tend to go with what comes easy.

You assume that going with your comfort level makes sense. In reality, your methods of avoidance only keep you from overcoming your anxiety. If you have a phobia about driving on freeways and get off the road every time you feel anxious, you prevent yourself from habituating to driving on freeways. The only way to overcome your phobia about driving on freeways is to get used to driving on freeways.

IDENTIFYING YOUR AVOIDANT BEHAVIORS

The first step in developing an exposure plan is to recognize your avoidant behaviors. This worksheet will be useful for your exposure exercises later in this chapter. At this point, consider how bad you feel about yourself as a result of escaping. It's an inefficient use of emotional energy. And what's more, in the long run, escaping makes your anxiety worse! You give yourself no chance to adjust to what triggered your anxiety and to minimize that fear. Therefore, identifying your fears and escape behaviors will be critical for defusing your anxiety.

Escape Behaviors

 Use this worksheet to identify your fears and the escape behaviors associated with them, as this will be critical for defusing your anxiety. I have filled in the first two lines to give you an example.

ESCAPE BEHAVIOR IDENTIFIER WORKSHEET

WHAT I FEAR	WHAT I DO TO ESCAPE IT
Meeting new people	Walk out of a room if a stranger enters
Crossing bridges	Pull over if there is a bridge ahead

Avoidance Behaviors

Now, let's identify your avoidance behaviors. Use the following worksheet to identify your fears and the avoidance behaviors associated with those fears. Remember that these are things you do to avoid anxiety-provoking situations before you even encounter them. This list of your avoidant behaviors will also be useful later when you move on to the exposure exercises. Although you might find it hard to believe now, you'll turn back to this list later for a perspective on how far you've come.

AVOIDANCE BEHAVIOR IDENTIFIER WORKSHEET

WHAT I FEAR	WHAT I DO TO AVOID IT
Meeting new people	Avoid social engagements of any kind.
Crossing bridges	Find a route to work with no bridges.

Procrastination

Procrastination is a tricky type of avoidance. You tell yourself that you aren't actually going to escape or avoid what you fear altogether. You tell yourself instead that you'll get to it later. But when? Usually it's at the last minute. Sometimes you wait so long that you must rush, which makes your performance sub par. When you procrastinate and perform poorly, you add to your stress and anxiety. Procrastination also heightens your anticipatory anxiety because you put off what you are dreading and hold back taking action. It's like pressing the gas pedal and the brakes at the same time.

Use the following worksheet to identify the types of situations that you fear and the ways you procrastinate. The "how" can be the kinds of rationalizations that you use. Finally, write down what usually results from the delay in your completing the task that you were postponing. This exercise illustrates how your procrastination increases, not decreases, your anxiety.

PROCRASTINATION IDENTIFIER WORKSHEET

FEAR	HOW I PROCRASTINATE	WHAT HAPPENS AS A RESULT
Talking to strangers	If a stranger comes into the room, I'll ignore him until he talks to me	My fear increases

This list will grow over time. This is because the ways you procrastinate are subtle and varied and can grow like weeds if you are prone to avoidance. Your responses to what happens when you procrastinate are particularly important to reflect upon. The anxiety you build when you avoid what you fear can be destructive.

Come back to this list over time and write down the new ways that you procrastinate. This task alone can help you minimize procrastination because you're becoming more aware of doing it. It can also motivate you to do it less often, because you must write it down and be accountable to yourself.

Safety Behaviors

Remember that safety behaviors are ways that you distract yourself when you are anxious. Initially, they can be useful to help you stay in a situation that makes you anxious. But the more you continue to use them, the more they become a method of avoiding your anxiety.

Identify your safety behaviors in the worksheet below. By identifying your safety behaviors, you can address these last vestiges of avoidance, which paradoxically increase your anxiety.

SAFETY BEHAVIOR IDENTIFIER WORKSHEET

FEAR	SAFETY BEHAVIOR
Talking to strangers in the supermarket	Pretending to talk on the cell phone

Some forms of distraction are useful at the beginning of an exposure exercise. For example, when you are attempting to conquer your fear of public speaking, it can be useful to focus on one person in the audience as a distraction. Later, you expand your attention to include the wider audience. But if safety behaviors continue, they outlive their usefulness. They make it difficult for you to habituate to anxiety-provoking situations. In addition to distracting you from the full experience of the exposure, you're reinforcing the idea that you need distraction because you aren't strong enough on your own to endure the experience.

Note How Your Avoidance Behaviors Have Increased

Now that you have identified the escape, avoidance, procrastination, and safety behaviors associated with your fears, it's time to take a look at how they have increased over time. Use the following worksheet to highlight how these behaviors have increased. First, identify your central fear(s). Then write down your most recent escape, avoidance, procrastination, and safety behaviors associated with that fear. Date them in the next column.

AVOIDANCE TIMELINE

FEAR	ESCAPE, AVOIDANCE, PROCRASTINATION, AND SAFETY BEHAVIORS	DATE
Dogs	Don't go to neighbor's house	1-5-13
	Give up walking outdoors	3-15-13

As you glance over this last worksheet, notice how your behaviors have slowly come to restrict your activities over time. Ask yourself: has your anxiety increased, along with the increase in your avoidance behaviors? The answer is probably yes. It's time to eliminate these behaviors, because they make things worse. They're like a wildfire that needs to be put out by cutting the brush and creating fire breaks.

Examine Your Fear Hierarchy

Finally, in the last worksheet before we move on to the exposure exercises, let's examine what your fears might be if you abandon your various forms of avoidance. In the first column, write down your worst fears. Start with the most extreme fear, then go to a lesser fear, and so on. Next, in the SUDS column, rate each fear according to the severity of distress you feel when experiencing it, 100 being the highest, and 1 being the lowest. Finish the worksheet by filling in the Forms of Avoidance and What Would Occur columns. The goal of this exercise is to think realistically about taking the first step toward exposure, which is to abandon avoidance.

FEAR HIERARCHY WORKSHEET

FEAR	SUDS SCORE	FORMS OF AVOIDANCE	WHAT WOULD OCCUR IF I ABANDON AVOIDANCE
Driving on the freeways	95	I drive on side roads, but sometimes it adds a few hours to my commute	I'll crash on the freeway

When you come back to this worksheet after you complete the exercises in the next section, you'll be struck by how unfounded your estimates are of what would occur if you abandon the forms of avoidance. Although you understand, now, that everything you have done to avoid anxiety has not worked for you, you have yet to experience the truth in this concept. That's where the exposure exercises come into play.

LEARNING TO RECONDITION YOURSELF

To recondition yourself, your job will be to avoid avoidance behaviors. In chapter 3, you learned that the amygdala does not lose its fear reactivity easily. You cannot deactivate your amygdala as if turning off a light switch. You must recondition it by exposing yourself repeatedly to what you fear until it becomes innocuous and you habituate to it.

The concept of conditioning has a long history. Every college student learns about Pavlov's dogs. More than 100 years ago, the Russian physiologist showed that, over a period of time, when he rang a bell and presented food together, he conditioned his dogs to expect that bells and food were related. Later, he rang the bell alone and found that the dogs salivated. This is called classical conditioning.

Fear and anxiety can be conditioned, too. A few years after Pavlov's experiments, American psychologist John Watson conditioned fear into a little boy who has since been referred to as "Little Albert." Watson presented a loud noise at the same time as a white, furry bunny and frightened little Albert. After a sufficient period of conditioning, Watson presented the white furry bunny without the loud noise. Albert became frightened by the bunny alone.

This classical conditioning paradigm can also be reversed. However, making the fear and anxiety go away through what has been called *extinction* (learning that nothing terrible actually happens) requires considerable time and repeated exposure. This is because the amygdala generalizes (it overreacts to anything remotely similar to your initial fear) and does not change its reactivity quickly. Simply deciding to change your anxiety level will not change it. That's only the first step. You need repeated exposures to make new learning possible in the amygdala. Repeated exposures include the fear-triggering stimulus (such as a white bunny, in the case of little Albert) and calming techniques, such as breathing and positive self-talk.

The key to reconditioning is to break the vicious avoidance cycle. You must also make sure that you expose yourself to what you were fearful of in the past. By keeping your behavioral options open to anxiety-provoking experiences, you allow yourself to be flexible and resilient to changing situations. By shifting to exposing yourself to what made you anxious in the past, you can learn to recondition yourself and habituate to that situation, event, or object.

Remember that making changes requires you to do things that initially feel foreign to you. You'll need to do things that you don't feel like doing. You'll also have to cut yourself off from all the escape and avoidant behaviors you identified in the last section. By eliminating the easy way out, you'll be able to take full advantage of the exposure exercises.

Yes, I mean full advantage. If you fully habituate to the experience, your brain will rewire. You need a moderate degree of anxiety to create neuroplasticity and rewire your brain. When you allow yourself only a low level of anxiety, such as when you give yourself an easy way out, you won't feel sufficient anxiety to make the exposure worthwhile. To make new connections between neurons, you need to be alert and motivated. Mild anxiety keeps you alert and motivated. Too little anxiety gets you bored. So, count on some anxiety. It'll be good for you.

Exposing Yourself to Life

Your life is what you make of it. Sure, there are things that you can't control. Your job is to respond adaptively to them. What you choose to do in life has a big effect on what you experience. For example, when I was twenty-two, I set off to travel west and returned a year later having never turned back east. I literally circled the globe, traveling through Asia, the Middle East, and Europe. Although this was a solo journey, I met many people along the way and encountered a wide range of situations, from the idyllic and exotic to the sad and tragic, including environments with extreme poverty and war zones.

Did I experience anxiety? Yes, but I managed my anxiety by choosing what to expose myself to and to what degree.

The key is that I was exposing myself to situations that *could* be anxiety-provoking but that didn't *have* to be anxiety-provoking. Because I chose to expose myself to those situations, I minimized my anxiety. In the years since that trip, I have taken many more excursions to challenging places. The point I am making is this: as you expose yourself to life, you teach yourself to manage anxiety and gain from exposing yourself to a range of experiences.

Of course you don't need to go to these travel extremes to neutralize anxiety. You can do a variety of things in your daily life to make exposure work for you.

Sandy Overcomes Her Fear of Flying

Sandy, a thirty-two-year-old flight attendant, developed a fear of flying after a near collision. To avert a disaster, the pilot abruptly dropped the plane in elevation by 1,000 feet (300 meters). Sandy had been walking in the aisle at the time and was thrown around the plane like a sack of potatoes. Although she was treated for bruises in the hospital, amazingly, she suffered no broken bones. She felt lucky to be alive. Sandy's face was bruised, however, so the airline gave her a few weeks off to recover. During that time, she and her family were surprised that she suffered no residual stress or nightmares.

Eventually, Sandy got a call from the airline to come back to work. She responded by saying that she wasn't ready to go back to work on an airplane. She offered to work checking in luggage, but the airline management rejected this idea. She responded by having a panic attack. After being given an ultimatum to return to work or be fired, Sandy came in to my mental health department for treatment. She demanded to see a psychiatrist and be given antianxiety medication. The psychiatrist gave her a prescription for Ativan.

Not long after the psychiatrist signed her disability forms, Sandy's life began to shrink. She withdrew from her usual range of activities and began to feel anxious about ordinary activities. For example, in addition to her fear of flying, she developed a fear of driving on freeways. Then she became anxious about driving in general. Her psychiatrist became concerned that she was regressing and sent her to my anxiety class.

Sandy said that it was "easier" to avoid anything that made her anxious. I told her that her avoidant behaviors were actually contributing to her anxiety and that she would eventually become agoraphobic if she continued to increase them. I explained that the anxious part of her brain, the amygdala, was essentially hijacking her frontal lobes. Because she was withdrawing, rather than confronting, her fears, she was shifting to a right frontal–lobe dominance, with its negative feelings, and underactivating her left frontal lobe, with its positive (can-do) feelings. She needed to take action, to activate her left frontal lobe. This description of what was happening in her brain seemed to make sense to her. In fact, she said, "This makes it tangible."

Despite getting the concept down, when we shifted to developing an exposure plan, she said that she wasn't quite sure if she was "ready" to begin right away and wanted to wait until she was feeling less anxious. I responded by telling her that her anxiety would actually increase if we waited, that waiting itself was an avoidant behavior.

Sandy began with driving on the freeway. Her hope was that I would be satisfied with having her drive on the freeway just one time. I told her that she would need to do it many times to promote neuroplasticity and habituation. Despite her anxiety, she complied, while practicing breathing techniques and self-talk.

When she returned a week later, she was proud to report that she had driven each of the previous days on the freeway and was feeling increasingly more confident about it. However, she didn't want to approach flying again until she had "built up her confidence." I again encouraged her to see that now was the time, and we developed a plan for gradual exposure. She began by going to the airport each day. Next, she walked up to the gates to say hello to colleagues. A week after that, with the aid of her colleagues, she entered an airplane. Next, she took a short flight, and then another. Soon, she was ready for a longer flight. All the while, she practiced breathing techniques, self-talk, and mindfulness meditation.

STEPS TO EXPOSURE

It's probable that you're frightened or apprehensive about the idea of exposing yourself to what you fear. Perhaps you worry that going through the exercises might make your condition worse. Or you might understand the *concept* of exposure, but you don't want to go through the discomfort of actual exposure. You are not alone if you fear doing these exercises. Many of the people attending my class are initially frightened to take the first step. But once they take the first step and discover what they achieve from the exercises, they become convinced that they are on the right track.

To ease your fears, consider this: there will be structure and gradations to these exercises. These evidence-based exercises have been used successfully with literally thousands of people who suffer from anxiety. They conquer their anxiety and learn to challenge themselves, which allows them to reap rewards from those challenges. Occasionally people relapse, but when they get back on the exposure program, they get better again.

The steps to the exposure exercises are as follows:

1. Identify your forms of avoidance. (You did this in the last section when you identified your escape, avoidant, procrastination, and safety behaviors.)
2. Use gradations in intensity of exposure. You'll start by using your imagination, then later using real-life exposure.
3. Eliminate your escape and avoidant behaviors.
4. Perform the easiest exposure first, then work up in difficulty.
5. Note the difference between your worst fears about exposure and what actually happened.
6. Note the gradual improvement in your symptoms.

Exposure Exercises

The gradations of exposure exercises begin in your imagination and move to real-life exposure. So, let's start with your imagination. In the worksheet below, write down things you fear and give them a SUDS score. Then, write down how you can imagine exposing yourself to the fear-generating situation *without* engaging in the escape and avoidant behaviors. For example, if the presence of a stranger yields a SUDS score of 50, write that down. Next, imagine being exposed to a stranger without escaping or avoiding the room. That might yield a SUDS score of 80. Repeat until your SUDS score drops to 20.

Try your own imagined exposure in the worksheet following the example. It's okay to use a form of distraction to begin with, but be sure you phase it out, so that you can reap the full rewards from the exposure. Practice your relaxation and cognitive restructuring exercises while practicing the exposure exercises. Make copies of the worksheets, so that you can practice the exposure exercises for all your fears.

IMAGINED EXPOSURE WORKSHEET EXAMPLE

FEAR	SUDS SCORE	ESCAPE OR AVOIDANT BEHAVIOR	IMAGINED EXPOSURE	SUDS AFTER EXPOSURE
Fear of strangers	50	I will leave the room	I will stay and listen to them	80
Fear of strangers	50	I will leave the room	I will stay and listen to them	71
Fear of strangers	50	I will leave the room	I will stay and listen to them	65
Fear of strangers	50	I will leave the room	I will stay and listen to them	31
Fear of strangers	50	I will leave the room	I will stay and listen to them	18

IMAGINED EXPOSURE WORKSHEET 1

FEAR	SUDS SCORE	ESCAPE OR AVOIDANT BEHAVIOR	IMAGINED EXPOSURE	SUDS AFTER EXPOSURE

Now, construct an imaginary exposure that makes your SUDs score higher than it is now. That's right, *higher.* You want to gradually work up to exposing yourself to experiences that triggered a high SUDS score. After a series of exposure exercises, your SUDS score will decrease. For example, let's say the avoidant behavior is staying away from people. Imagine yourself approaching a roomful of strangers, without escaping or moving to the back of the room. Next, imagine yourself approaching someone you don't know and introducing yourself. Note your degree of anxiety in the SUDS column. Now, ask polite questions of the stranger. Repeat this imaginary exposure exercise until your SUDS score falls to 20. Remember to eliminate your escape and avoidant behaviors.

IMAGINED EXPOSURE WORKSHEET 2

FEAR	SUDS SCORE	ESCAPE OR AVOIDANT BEHAVIOR	IMAGINED EXPOSURE	SUDS AFTER EXPOSURE

Notice the differences between your SUDS scores before and after repeated imaginary exposures. The point to learn from these exercises is that after repeated exposures, your anxiety decreases.

One of the techniques of successful exposure is to accept the experience at all levels. This means that instead of gritting your teeth (a safety behavior), you fully expose yourself to the situation and observe yourself doing it. This technique allows you to *decenter* the anxiety-provoking effect. You are essentially stepping back from resisting any anxiety and allowing yourself to go through the experience. You're stepping back from the fight. This helps you be a detached observer, rather than a person trying to avoid being anxious.

This may seem like a subtle point. But consider for a moment what happens when you detach and become an observer. Instead of investing your energy in trying to avoid what makes you anxious, you're allowing your observing skills to take center stage. When you're engaging in avoidant behaviors, the anxiety and your avoidance of it takes all your attention. By taking a step back and accepting the experience, you become an observer, which enlarges your perspective. You become more than a person who is trying to stay away from anxiety.

Real-Life Exposure

Real-life exposure is considerably more powerful than imagery exposure. Sometimes referred to as *in vivo* exposure, real-life exposures involve putting yourself in the situations that you fear. Consider the imagery exercises you just performed a step toward real-life (in vivo) exposure. In vivo exposure entails actually approaching a real roomful of people you have never met. Each time you perform this exercise, you increase your contact with others. Eventually, you walk up and introduce yourself to someone you don't know. Whatever method you use (imaginary or in vivo), the exposure should be graduated in intensity and never retreating.

Certainly, real-life exposure is more difficult than imagined exposure. It can be difficult even for those without anxiety disorders to face their fears. Try not to get discouraged. In fact, remind yourself while doing the exposure exercises that the more difficulty you have with the exposure exercise, the more effective it will be. Remember, too, that you have already performed the imagined exercises, so you already have a head start. Take your exposures in steps. Use your worksheet on short-term and long-term goals from chapter 7, and practice setting short-term goals to reach your long-term goal.

Amanda Sets Goals to Overcome Her Bridge Phobia

Amanda came to see me because she took a job in San Francisco just south of where she lived. Her commute to work included driving across the Golden Gate Bridge daily, which frightened her horribly. The Golden Gate Bridge, in contrast to the other bridges in the Bay Area, features cross traffic, and head-on accidents on the bridge are not uncommon. Sometimes, these accidents occur when a driver gazes out at the spectacular view or at the pedestrians strolling on the walkway and swerves into the oncoming lane. When Amanda used these infrequent accidents as a reason for avoiding driving across the bridge, I told her that I always avoid driving in the lane closest to oncoming traffic because of the accident potential, then enjoy the drive. She responded by saying, "I could fall off the side if I was too far over to the right."

Despite her catastrophic thinking, Amanda agreed to work together to develop a number of short-term goals in service of her long-term goal of driving across the bridge. To start with, Amanda used imagined exposure, then, after reaching a 20 SUDS score, she moved on to an in vivo exposure. First, she walked across the bridge until her score went down to a 20 SUDS score. She then graduated to taking a bus, and after reaching a 20 SUDS score at that, she moved on to being a passenger in a car. Finally, she drove across the bridge by herself, repeating the exposure until her SUDS score dropped to 20.

Here is Amanda's exposure worksheet. Her long-term goal is to drive across the Golden Gate Bridge.

AMANDA'S IN VIVO EXPOSURE WORKSHEET

SHORT-TERM GOALS	FEAR	REALISTIC APPRAISAL AND COPING SKILLS	SUDS AFTER EXPOSURE
Imagined driving across the bridge	I'll be killed in a head-on accident	I'm in the far right lane, and no one can hit me	70
	There will be another accident	The chances of an accident are extremely slim	20
Walking across the bridge	I will fall off into the sea	The guardrail is high, and I stay way from it, anyway	60
	Someone will push me over	No one is stupid enough 15 to do it in public	15
Taking a bus across the bridge	The bus will crash	I'll be safe in it, even if the improbable were to happen	55
	The bus will swerve off the side	The driver isn't that crazy	11
Being a passenger	A car will hit us head-on	We will be in the far right lane	68
	My friend will lose concentration and cause an accident	She is a great driver, and I won't distract her	19
Driving across the bridg	A car will swerve over and hit me	I have learned to drive in the right lane and be alert	79
	The car in front of me will slam on its brakes	The chances of that happening are rare	55
	There will be a pile-up	It's rare, and I'll be fine	33
	My car will swerve off	I will drive cautiously	22

Identify Your Short-Term and Long-Term Exposure Goals

Use the following worksheet to monitor your graduated and sequential exposures. Just like Amanda, structure your short-term exposure goals, so they lead you to accomplish your long-term goal. After your SUDS score goes down to 20, move to the next short-term goal (a more difficult exposure). Be sure to reach a 20 SUDS score before going to the next short-term exposure goal.

IN VIVO EXPOSURE WORKSHEET

SHORT-TERM GOALS	FEAR	REALISTIC APPRAISAL AND COPING SKILLS	SUDS

Good job! Repeat this exercise many times. The more you repeat it, the less anxiety you'll experience. Remember to use your coping techniques, such as breathing and self-talk, each time.

Steven Uses Exposure to Expand His World

Steven had been married for six years and had a four-year-old son. His wife requested that he come in to be evaluated and treated. When I asked Steven why his wife wanted him to come in, he responded, "I think she wants me out more." Only after considerable encouragement to be more revealing did he tell me that, over the past few years, he had been gradually withdrawing to limit his activities to home and work. It was only after his wife threatened to leave him because he wanted to quit his job that he sought treatment.

Steven noted that he had always been a worrier, but, in recent years, he found that the number of situations that made him feel overwhelmingly anxious had grown. He withdrew in response to this increase in anxiety. At work, he sometimes got up abruptly and left a meeting if he felt anxious. Often, he avoided going into the conference room or break room, for fear of getting involved in a conversation. Some of his peers had begun to say, "What's up, Steve?" He didn't know what to say.

After a few weeks of practicing the skills you're learning, Steven found that his general level of free-floating anxiety had subsided. As a first step toward the exposure exercise, he completed the worksheets on identifying his escape, avoidant, procrastination, and safety behaviors. He was amazed by how many he had and how they had increased over time. Next, he began the imagined exposures, followed by the in vivo exercises.

Steven started his exposure exercises by imagining going into the break room at work. First, he simply stood there and listened to others. Then, he imagined striking up a conversation. He followed the imagined exercise with real-life exposure by first entering the break room, then approaching one of his colleagues to ask a question, then finally striking up a conversation.

Over the next few weeks, Steven worked hard to develop new behaviors that surprised his coworkers. And he was delighted to report that his wife praised him for saying that he intended to stick it out at work.

Up Your Exposure Intensity

Use the following worksheet to chart the progress of your exposures. Write down the type of exposure in the first column (note whether it is imagined or in vivo), then note the symptoms you experienced. Next, give yourself a SUDS score and describe the coping techniques you used. Finally, write down your plan for the next exposure.

For this exposure, increase the time period or the intensity of it. The point here is that you want to dose yourself with ever-increasing amounts of what you had found intolerable in the past. For example, let's return to Amanda's bridge phobia. With imagined exposure, she can have the traffic come to a halt, or she can turn around and drive back over the bridge again. In fact, Amanda did turn around after crossing the bridge and drove across again. This helped her habituate to the experience of driving across the bridge. The more she did it, the more at ease she was the next time.

Perform your exposures until your SUDS goes down to 20. Then up the intensity and repeat the exposure until your SUDS again goes down to 20. Each time, note the coping skills that you used and the plan to modify those coping skills for the next exposure.

SUDS EXPOSURE WORKSHEET

TYPE OF EXPOSURE	SYMPTOMS	SUDS	COPING SKILL	PLAN FOR THE NEXT EXPOSURE

Notice how the symptoms change with each exposure. Similarly, watch how your SUDS score changes. At the end of the sheet, you'll notice that, although the intensities of the exposures increased, your SUDS score eventually decreased. This exercise represents a fundamental truth about anxiety: The more you expose yourself to the things and situations you fear, the less anxiety you will suffer. Because avoidant behaviors increase your anxiety, your treatment should include exposure. There is no way to escape this fact, so practice the exercises in this chapter often.

Chapter 9
Accepting Your Bodily Sensations

In the preceding chapters, you learned that mistaken beliefs frame what you avoid with fear and that avoidance behaviors lead to more anxiety. You learned how to change your mistaken beliefs and avoid avoidance. Now, you're ready to take the next step. You will actually induce some of the physical sensations associated with anxiety and panic, so that you can habituate to them and neutralize their negative effects.

Because you have been working to change your automatic thoughts, assumptions, and core beliefs and have learned relaxation exercises, as well as breathing and positive self-talk, you're now better able to cope with and adapt to the physical sensations you overreacted to in the past. Your new thinking skills have helped you understand that your physical sensations are nothing to be alarmed about. Now, your thoughts and emotions need to be integrated positively with your physical sensations. Because your thoughts often lead the way, and your emotions eventually follow, integrating positive thoughts are important when experiencing the bodily sensations you have been avoiding like the plague.

In this chapter, you'll learn the skills necessary to accept the physical sensations associated with anxiety and panic, so that they can fade into the background and won't continue to demand your attention. You'll learn:

- why it's important to face your physical sensations.
- that your physical sensations are not dangerous.
- how overreacting to physical sensations leads to panic.
- to break the panic cycle by riding out the physical sensations.
- how to use interoceptive exposure to habituate to your physical sensations.

ANXIETY SENSITIVITY

These physical sensations are common to people familiar with anxiety and panic:

- lightheadedness
- dizziness
- blurred vision
- cold hands
- muscle weakness
- heart palpitations
- feeling like you're not getting enough air
- numbness or tingling

- sweating
- difficulty focusing your thoughts
- choking
- shaking or trembling
- hot flashes
- nausea
- chest pain

Do you experience symptoms that are different from those in the previous list? What are they? Write them down below.

WHAT ARE YOUR ANXIETY SYMPTOMS?

_____   _____

_____   _____

_____   _____

_____   _____

_____   _____

One of the factors that contributes to avoidant behaviors is referred to as *anxiety sensitivity*. If you think that any anxiety is bad and must be avoided, you cultivate anxiety sensitivity—you become hypersensitive to the sensations that you assume signal danger ahead. They are actually false alarms.

Here's how it works: Let's say you are anxious in social situations. You decide that you will engage in social situations only when you are free of anxiety, because you don't want others to know that you are anxious. Each time you experience some anxiety, you experience it in an all-or-nothing way. Although there are actually degrees of anxiety, when you're stuck in an all-or-nothing mode, a little feels like a lot. A little anxiety in a social situation becomes intolerable, because even a little anxiety is too much to handle. So you avoid similar situations. Then other situations that are the slightest bit social make you anxious, just by thinking about them. Soon the physical sensations that you associate with anxiety occur without provocation. When you try to avoid those sensations, your anxiety sensitivity increases. And, most important, your anxiety level increases because you fear the physical sensations.

Doug fell into this trap. He began feeling a tightness in his chest and some constriction in his throat. When he felt these sensations, he began to have trouble swallowing and began to breath quickly. Then, his heart started to race and he began to panic. Soon, Doug began to monitor and fear feeling tightness in his chest. Even a little tightness became too much tightness. He did whatever he could to minimize any chance of feeling this sensation.

Dr. David Barlow from Boston University pointed out the importance of differentiating between false alarms and real alarms. False alarms are learned (conditioned) alarms. A false alarm is like Doug's feeling of tightness in his chest. When he felt his chest become tight, the alarm went off that something terrible was going to happen, and he began to panic.

But nothing terrible did happen, so the alarm wasn't real. When you avoid dealing with learned alarms, they can strengthen and become resistant to extinction.

ACKNOWLEDGING YOUR BODILY SENSATIONS

A paradox occurs when you try to avoid your physical sensations. When you try really hard *not* to feel something, you'll feel it even more. For example, try really hard to *not* sense the weight of this book in your hands. Try to block out those sensations! Because I brought the feel of this book to your attention and asked you to try hard to keep those sensations *out* of your mind, you noticed them even more.

A funny thing happens when you stop trying. Once you acknowledge and simply observe the sensations of the book's weight and feel, they fade into the background. This is the principle used in many chronic pain programs. Chronic pain patients learn to stop trying to avoid or block out the physical sensations of pain and instead observe and accept them. This can be frightening for people who have been traumatized by debilitating pain. Why face terrible pain when they have had too much of it already? The answer is that by accepting the pain, it actually fades. This is one step toward making chronic pain tolerable. The same principle applies to the physical sensations you associate with anxiety. You want to stop trying *not* to feel those sensations. Instead, observe and accept them.

The key to accepting your physical sensations and turning off the false alarms is to shift from yes-versus-no, black-versus-white, and all-or-nothing frames of reference. Trying to feel *no* physical sensations, such as sweaty palms, for example, makes even slightly sweating palms feel like they're dripping wet. It's like a pendulum. The farther you push it one way, the farther back it will swing. The harder you try to push your sweaty palms out of your mind, the sweatier they become. As you become anxious about the physical sensations, your anxiety increases. The way out of this vicious cycle is to shift from the all-or-nothing perspective to a detached-observer perspective and simply note that your palms are sweating. Eventually, they'll dry out.

The more you fear the physical symptoms of anxiety and panic, the more you become hypervigilant about them, and even normal bodily sensations become alarming. Doug's fear of the tightness in his chest increased his anxiety. He began to fear other sensations, as well, which soon spurred panic attacks. This panic cycle is self-perpetuating. Here is a typical panic cycle:

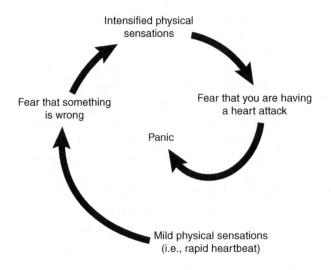

You can break this cycle at any point along the way. Because the physical sensations can be false alarms, you'll need to learn to detach yourself from them and ride them out. That's where shifting away from the all-or-nothing frame of reference comes into play. By learning to accept your physical sensations, you put out the fire before you can pour gasoline on it.

LEARNING INTEROCEPTIVE EXPOSURE

Panic disorder results from being phobic about your own bodily sensations. Just as Doug became phobic about tightness in his chest, you can become phobic about physical sensations such as shortness of breath, a dry throat, or dizziness. If you suffer from panic attacks, you likely are constantly monitoring your body for any physical sensation that might "warn" you that an attack is on the way. You try to "make sure nothing terrible happens." So you avoid doing anything that might stir up those bodily sensations, such as jogging, running up the stairs, or playing games that require a lot of physical exertion.

Panic attacks come seemingly out of the blue. They occur when you suddenly feel physical sensations that you fear. Consequently, you have a tendency to try to control the conditions in which these sensations occur. Because avoiding what you fear leads to the temporary belief that you are in control, your avoidance behaviors will probably increase. Yet, the physical sensations always seem to be around the next corner. You might even feel that they're chasing you. So, you try to keep one step ahead of them by avoiding even *more* things that could bring them on again. There is a very basic problem with this: These sensations are not dangerous! They are dangerous only in your mind.

As you learned in the last chapter, the more you avoid what you fear, the more you will fear it. Avoiding fears is a short-term solution that creates a long-term problem and results in anxiety, phobias, and panic attacks. Avoidance essentially gets your amygdala over-sensitized to minor sensations. Then, your frontal lobes narrow your attention to warning signals that are really false alarms. For example, if, like Doug, you fear the sensation of your chest tightening, any semblance of a tight chest will activate your amygdala.

The way out of this trap is to become used to those physical sensations, so that they don't trigger false alarms and result in panic attacks. You conditioned yourself to respond to these sensations as if they were of "alarming importance." Now, you must "de-condition" yourself to them, so that they are just like any other sensations. Now that you understand this important principle, we can move to the technique called *interoceptive exposure,* which will help you habituate to your own bodily sensations, so that they won't frighten you.

Anxiety specialists such as Drs. Barlow, Craske, and Zuercher-White point out that there are two main sources of fear that generate anxiety disorders: extroceptive and interoceptive. Extroceptive fear is about something outside of you. Interoceptive fear is about something inside of you. Extroceptive fear occurs when you overreact to feared objects or situations. For example, in social phobia, extroceptive fear occurs when you stand in front of a group of people giving a presentation. Interoceptive fear refers to your reactions to internal sensations, such as the physical sensations that occur when you stand in front of those people: a dry mouth, sweating, and butterflies in your stomach.

Interoceptive exposure is a process of systematically desensitizing yourself to those physical sensations; it helps you habituate to them. During interoceptive exposure, you restructure your thinking, using positive self-talk and narratives, while experiencing the physical sensations that arise. Developing new automatic thoughts and assumptions during interoceptive exposure exercises helps you gain confidence and learn to ride out those physical sensations, so they eventually become innocuous.

Remember, the goal is not to eliminate anxiety but to reduce it and make it more manageable. Anxiety is a necessary part of life that can be used to keep you constructively alert and motivated.

Becoming Comfortable in Your Own Skin

Normally, a person without panic disorder appraises activated physical sensations, such as rapid heartbeat and shortness of breath, as innocuous. A realistic assessment of the potential danger of an anxiety-provoking situation derails the fight-or-flight response from being triggered. The brain's hippocampus accesses memories and context that allow for such thoughts as, "Oh yes, I've had shortness of breath and a rapid heartbeat before. Nothing bad happened."

Some researchers, including Dr. Albert Bandura of Stanford University, have pointed out that believing in your ability to succeed is the most important factor operating in anxiety disorders. If you think that you are unable to cope with anxiety in what you assume to be a potentially threatening situation, your anxiety increases. When you develop self-confidence, your anxiety decreases. In other words, when you believe that you are able to deal with the situation, your anxiety level goes down. When you observe and accept the physical sensations that arise, your sense of mastery over them makes your anxiety fade.

Bandura cites well-known studies that involved administering epinephrine (adrenaline) to subjects who were led to believe that they were either in a positive (controllable) or negative (uncontrollable) situation. Those who believed that they were in an uncontrollable situation experienced increased anxiety from the epinephrine. Those who were led to believe that they were in a controllable situation reported great pleasure. The point is that a shot of adrenaline doesn't necessarily lead to anxiety. It's all in how you interpret the sensations. If you interpret the physical sensations positively, or at least as a neutral experience, you won't be plagued by anxiety.

Because your previous response to the physical sensations was to avoid them, what I am about to propose may seem counterintuitive. *If you invite, accept, and do not resist your physical sensations, you will defuse, disarm, and diminish their negative effect.* What you'll learn to do is the opposite of what you feel is safe.

As a first step toward learning interoceptive exposure, let's examine your current automatic physical sensations. In the left-hand column, write down the physical sensations that apply to you. These physical sensations can include sweaty palms, rapid heartbeat, and shallow breathing, among others. In the right-hand column, write down your usual response to these sensations.

ASSESS YOUR PHYSICAL SENSATIONS

PHYSICAL SENSATIONS	RESPONSES
Shortness of breath	*I breathe harder to get more air*

Now that you have identified what your usual responses are to physical sensations, it's time to practice your coping skills. Use the following worksheet to identify the physical sensations and the newly learned skills you will use to cope with each one. This exercise will help you remember to use your coping skills.

IDENTIFY YOUR COPING SKILLS

PHYSICAL SENSATIONS	RESPONSES
Shortness of breath	*I'll breathe abdominally*

Practice Your Coping Skills

The next step is to actually bring on the physical sensations and try out your coping skills. This shift requires that you move toward, not away from, the physical sensations that make you anxious.

This probably sounds like a frightening challenge. But don't forget that rewiring your brain requires that you do what you don't want to do. If you do what you feel like doing, you'll continue strengthening old habits. We generally do what comes easily, and the more we do those things, the more we will do them again and the more they will eventually come easily. Change requires forcing yourself to establish new habits, especially when your old habits include avoiding discomfort.

An Elevating Opportunity

I wrote the following paragraphs while stuck in an elevator in a Washington D.C. hotel (truly!). If I had been plagued by anxiety, I would have reacted to this experience with panic. But I decided to use this as an opportunity instead.

It is hot in here, and there's little air to breathe. I am sweating profusely. Yet, I am not experiencing any anxiety because these physiological symptoms do not press the alarm button for me. Neither does the situation. I'm not trying to act macho by saying this. Rather, I am illustrating the point that we react to what we interpret as dangerous. This situation, for me, is not.

I can hear the fire department working to open the door. I don't know how long it will take before they succeed. I can make this experience intolerable, or I can cope with it. I'm coping with it, not by distracting myself, but by focusing on the experience itself.

I'm observing that it is getting warmer, and the air is getting even more stale. I'm sweating, despite becoming dehydrated. This is a forced exposure exercise that includes one physiological sensation I have grown to dislike,

dehydration. But I know that I can simply observe and accept these sensations. As I listen to the rescue crew yell to one another in frustration that it is taking longer than they expected, I can assume that I will be stuck in here for many hours, or I could just accept whatever happens. I will go with the latter because this is the only reasonable choice. Why fight what I cannot control?

Just as I'm doing now, your job is to turn each experience into a positive. I turned this into an opportunity to write a little sidebar for this book. Each situation can yield its own opportunities. By shifting to acceptance and observance, you permit yourself to make your experiences positive.

They're now yelling to me, "Are you all right?"

I yell back, "Take your time. I'm fine."

A few minutes go by, and they open the doors. I jump out of my writing chamber and thank them for their help. Secretly, I thank them for the opportunity to write this section.

Preparing for the Exercises

In the following pages, you will be using a variety of methods to induce the physical sensations you fear. It's time to gain mastery over these false alarms. You'll soon learn to habituate to the physical symptoms to which you've been overreacting.

Listed below are some things that will be useful to have available for the exercises, along with some things to keep in mind as you prepare for the exercises.

- Use the worksheets in this chapter to help demonstrate gains as you practice the interoceptive exposure exercises.

- In addition to the worksheets, you might need the following items: a timer, a pencil, and a straw.

- There is a major difference between anxiety and sensation intensity. Anxiety is uncomfortable at best and frightening at worst. Sensation intensity (shortness of breath and dizziness) need only be uncomfortable at its worst. To see this difference, observe your SUDS score go down, despite the physical discomfort.

- Some people like to have a coach available (a friend or family member) to give encouragement. You may want the coach to do the exercises with you.

- It's common to experience anxiety and/or panic the first few times you perform the exercises. This a great opportunity to practice the anxiety-reduction techniques you learned in the previous chapters. You need practice!

- Allow yourself to fully experience the symptoms. Trust your ability to succeed. The idea is to habituate to the sensations. You want the full benefit of the exposure.

- Keep doing the exercises until you get your SUDS down to 20.

- The exposures should be regular and graduated in intensity, versus sporadic and intense. In other words, you'll need to do them often and increase the difficulty level steadily. Don't practice sporadically, and then try to make up for lost time by going from 0 to 60 in intensity.

- Apply coping skills, such as abdominal breathing and positive self-talk, during the exposure exercises. Say to yourself, "Oh, this rapid heartbeat is no big thing. I've experienced it many times, and nothing terrible happened."

- Stay focused, to maximize the involvement of your frontal lobes and memory, so you can allow yourself to increase self-efficacy during the exposure. Pay attention and observe yourself as you perform the exposure.

The interoceptive exercises include:

- overbreathing
- running in place
- holding your breath
- spinning
- swallowing quickly
- tensing your body
- standing up quickly from lying on the floor
- staring at one spot
- shaking your head from side to side
- putting your head between your legs, then sitting up

There are a few exclusions for these exercises. If you are pregnant or have asthma, a heart condition, low blood pressure, or epilepsy, don't engage in these exercises. Ask your doctor whether these exercises put your medical situation at risk. Overall, however, most people without these conditions should be able to perform these exercises without risk.

Using the Worksheets

The worksheets that follow are designed to demonstrate your progress and to show you how you can improve. Each of the exposures, such as spinning or overbreathing, should be performed repeatedly and as instructed. Don't forget that the physical symptoms are not dangerous! Getting your heart rate up, for example, will not cause a heart attack, hyperventilating will not cause you to pass out, and swallowing quickly won't make you choke to death. For each worksheet:

- Jot down your symptoms.
- Give them a SUDS score.
- Write down your worse fear(s).
- Estimate the odds that it will happen.
- Note whether your worst fear occurred: Y/N.
- Write down what you did to cope.

After each exercise, I'll describe what Carol, a person who attended my class, said about the exercises, so that you can see how someone else reacted. Not everyone responds in the same way. So if your reaction is different, there's nothing to be worried about. Your goal is to repeat each exercise until your SUDS score goes down to 20. Don't try to do them all in one day, at one go. Carol performed each of these exercises over a period of weeks, then practiced them at home between classes.

Overbreathing leads to lightheadedness and rapid heartbeat. This overbreathing exercise can illustrate how to unlink hyperventilation and panic. Your task is to hyperventilate by breathing quickly, with an emphasis on the exhale, for 1½ minutes. Alternatively, you can breathe through a straw for 1 minute. Hold your nose while breathing through the straw, and try to get as much air as you can.

OVERBREATHING WORKSHEET

EXERCISES	DESCRIBE YOUR SYMPTOMS	SUDS	WORST FEAR	ODDS OF THIS HAPPENING	DID IT HAPPEN?	YOUR COPING SKILLS
Trial #1						
Trial #2						
Trial #3						
Trial #4						
Trial #5						
Trial #6						
Trial #7						
Trial #8						
Trial #9						
Trial #10						

Carol described her physical symptoms after the overbreathing exercise like this: "That got my heart racing, and my mind was right behind it." She also said that she started sweating and felt dizzy. Her hands shook, and her throat went dry. She gave it a 98 on the SUDS for the first trial.

During trial number 2, it went down to 81. Her mind did not race, but her heart rate remained high. After trial number 3, her SUDS score went down to 63. She was amazed that it was getting easier. On trial 5, she said, "I'm getting the hang of it now. I'd say this is a 20. Maybe less!"

Jog in place vigorously for 1 minute, to increase your heart rate and cause hyperventilation. Of course, how intensely your heart races and how hard you breathe are reflections of how fit you are. Base how intensely you jog on how much physical exertion you can expend. You want your heart rate up! Don't forget that an increased heart rate is nothing to panic about.

RUNNING IN PLACE WORKSHEET

EXERCISES	DESCRIBE YOUR SYMPTOMS	SUDS	WORST FEAR	ODDS OF THIS HAPPENING	DID IT HAPPEN?	YOUR COPING SKILLS
Trial #1						
Trial #2						
Trial #3						
Trial #4						
Trial #5						
Trial #6						
Trial #7						
Trial #8						
Trial #9						
Trial #10						

After trial number 1 of this exercise, Carol said, "I'm out of shape. My heart started racing, and I couldn't get enough air!" As she caught her breath, she said that her thoughts also began to race. She wondered whether she did damage to her heart. She wrote down 95 for her SUDS. I reminded her of the changes she had made in her automatic thoughts, assumptions, and core beliefs—moving from negative to positive. "I feel tired—that's bad" changed to "Feeling tired is okay." She also changed her assumptions, from "I'm tired, I could have a heart attack" to "This feeling of tiredness is good. I'll sleep well tonight." And, finally, her core belief shifted from "I'm so out of shape that I'll never be able to get back in shape" to "I'm a healthy person and can get in better shape."

Abdominal breathing helped slow her breathing rate down. After waiting about 5 minutes, she tried the exercise again, and it got easier. Although she rated trial number 2 a 72, she did not have the catastrophic thoughts about damaging her heart. With trial 3, her SUDS dropped to 51. On trial 4, it went down to 8, and she felt no anxiety symptoms.

Hold your breath for 30 seconds. This tightens the chest and leads to a sense of suffocation. This exercise probably sounds like an odd one to induce the physical sensations associated with anxious feelings. But tightness in your chest and the accompanying sense of suffocation can cause you to gasp for air and begin to breathe quickly to compensate. This can lead to a variety of symptoms that can trigger a false alarm and cascade into panic. By practicing this exposure, you can shift this sensation from being a trigger for a panic attack to simply an innocuous sensation.

BREATH-HOLDING WORKSHEET

EXERCISES	DESCRIBE YOUR SYMPTOMS	SUDS	WORST FEAR	ODDS OF THIS HAPPENING	DID IT HAPPEN?	YOUR COPING SKILLS
Trial #1						
Trial #2						
Trial #3						
Trial #4						
Trial #5						
Trial #6						
Trial #7						
Trial #8						
Trial #9						
Trial #10						

After holding her breath for trial number 1, Carol said, "That forced me to start breathing fast, and that got my heart pumping, too!" She rated it an 80 and worried that she had damaged her lungs. But that fear quickly faded. Trial number 2 was easier. She didn't resort to breathing quickly, and her heart rate was stable. For trial number 3, she decided to see whether she could hold her breath for longer than the 30 seconds. This got her heart rate up again, and her breathing quickened as she gasped for air. Her SUDS score rose to 80. She was quite relieved when her SUDS score for the next few trials dropped quickly.

 Spin around, either while standing or in a swivel chair by pushing around with your feet. After spinning, attempt walking. The most common symptom of spinning is dizziness.

Some people feel dizzier than others. Other common symptoms include nausea and blurry vision. Don't forget that dizziness is nothing to panic about.

SPINNING WORKSHEET

EXERCISES	DESCRIBE YOUR SYMPTOMS	SUDS	WORST FEAR	ODDS OF THIS HAPPENING	DID IT HAPPEN?	YOUR COPING SKILLS
Trial #1						
Trial #2						
Trial #3						

Trial #4						
Trial #5						
Trial #6						
Trial #7						
Trial #8						
Trial #9						
Trial #10						

After trial number 1 of the spinning exercise Carol said, "That got me dizzy too quickly. My vision is blurry. I feel nauseous." She had to wait a few minutes before trying it again. After trial number 2, she explained that she got dizzy on rides at amusement parks and her nausea would often linger for hours. We decided that she would move on to the next exercise without any more trials.

Swallow quickly four times in a row. This can cause you to feel a lump in your throat. Some people wonder what swallowing could possibly have to do with anxiety. Others know all too well that a dry throat and an interruption in their breathing can trigger other symptoms that they fear. Swallowing quickly, having a dry throat, and feeling a lump in your throat are normal sensations, and your task is to learn to react to those sensations as normal feelings.

SWALLOWING WORKSHEET

EXERCISES	DESCRIBE YOUR SYMPTOMS	SUDS	WORST FEAR	ODDS OF THIS HAPPENING	DID IT HAPPEN?	YOUR COPING SKILLS
Trial #1						
Trial #2						
Trial #3						
Trial #4						
Trial #5						
Trial #6						
Trial #7						
Trial #8						
Trial #9						
Trial #10						

Carol kept on swallowing after the initial four times. This disrupted her breathing pattern, and she stood up abruptly, as if that would clear her throat. She looked at me, wondering how to stop swallowing. She gave her first trial a SUDS score of 80. She went on for ten more swallows, fearing that she couldn't stop. Trial number 2 was easier for her. She stopped at four swallows without a problem.

While sitting, tense your entire body, making fists and bringing your shoulders forward. Tighten your chest and entire body. Body tension can trigger a false alarm because during periods of anxiety your body can tense up. The associations that you make when you tense up can unconsciously remind you of feeling anxious. But they need not lead to anxiety. In this exercise, you'll learn to make sure that they don't.

BODY TENSION WORKSHEET

EXERCISES	DESCRIBE YOUR SYMPTOMS	SUDS	WORST FEAR	ODDS OF THIS HAPPENING	DID IT HAPPEN?	YOUR COPING SKILLS
Trial #1						
Trial #2						
Trial #3						
Trial #4						
Trial #5						
Trial #6						
Trial #7						
Trial #8						
Trial #9						
Trial #10						

Carol said, "Oh, I don't know how I'm going to get my body any tenser." Her worst fear was that she would make her muscles spasm, then have a heart attack or seizures and die. She rated trial number 1 at 95. "I felt like my body locked up! Why did you ask me to do that?"

She was able to loosen up after a few moments of constricted breathing and feeling that she was trapped in her own body. After trials 2, 3, 4, and 5, she loosened up more quickly and rated her SUDS at 80, 71, 50, and 33, respectively. She said, "You know, that's a funny way to relax. I think I'll do it more often."

Standing up quickly from lying on the floor can cause dizziness. You might also find yourself becoming a little nauseous and blurry-eyed, sensations that can lead to panic. Standing up quickly is something you'll do throughout your life. This will help you get used to the temporary dizziness and other sensations that result from it. If you have low blood pressure, this exercise can be particularly difficult; you might want to skip it.

STANDING UP WORKSHEET

EXERCISES	DESCRIBE YOUR SYMPTOMS	SUDS	WORST FEAR	ODDS OF THIS HAPPENING	DID IT HAPPEN?	YOUR COPING SKILLS
Trial #1						
Trial #2						

Trial #3					
Trial #4					
Trial #5					
Trial #6					
Trial #7					
Trial #8					
Trial #9					
Trial #10					

Carol said she had bad knees and that it would be difficult to perform this exercise. Her worst fear was that she would injure her knees or back. Nevertheless, she tried it. To her surprise, her knees and back were fine, but she was dizzy, and her vision was blurry. "I feel lightheaded, like I'm going to faint." She gave the first trial a SUDS of 90. By trial number 6, the dizziness had passed, and her SUDS was down to 20. She said, "Maybe this will end up strengthening my knees, instead of hurting them!"

Pick a spot on a blank wall and stare at it without deviation for 2 minutes. This can simulate the feeling of being trapped. Those with claustrophobia might find this exercise particularly troublesome. Try to keep at it, though; in the long run, it can help you lessen the effects of claustrophobia. The feeling of being confused and trapped can trigger anxiety and the need to look away as a means to calm yourself down. Resist this temptation. Remember we want to stir up disturbing sensations, so that you can eventually habituate to them.

STARING WORKSHEET

EXERCISES	DESCRIBE YOUR SYMPTOMS	SUDS	WORST FEAR	ODDS OF THIS HAPPENING	DID IT HAPPEN?	YOUR COPING SKILLS
Trial #1						
Trial #2						
Trial #3						
Trial #4						
Trial #5						
Trial #6						
Trial #7						
Trial #8						
Trial #9						
Trial #10						

The idea of staring at a spot on the wall as an anxiety exercise struck Carol as a joke. However, as she was getting ready for the first trial, she asked, "What if I need to look away?" I told her that this was the point—she can't. She reflected anxiously for a moment. "What if something happens?"

She rated trial number 1 an 87 on the SUDS scale. She reported that her heart started racing, and she started hyperventilating. On trial number 2, she found herself beginning to relax. Her SUDS score went down to 70. By trial number 4, she was down to 20 with no symptoms and said, "That was kind of a meditative exercise."

 Set a timer for 1½ minutes. Shake your head from side to side. Lower your head and shift it from side to side. When the timer goes off after 1½ minutes, raise your head. This exercise is similar to the standing-up exercise, in that one of the most common symptoms is dizziness, followed by blurry vision. Think of it as a good neck exercise, but do it slowly so you don't pull a muscle. Don't forget that you want to induce uncomfortable sensations so that you can habituate to them.

SHAKING YOUR HEAD WORKSHEET

EXERCISES	DESCRIBE YOUR SYMPTOMS	SUDS	WORST FEAR	ODDS OF THIS HAPPENING	DID IT HAPPEN?	YOUR COPING SKILLS
Trial #1						
Trial #2						
Trial #3						
Trial #4						
Trial #5						
Trial #6						
Trial #7						
Trial #8						
Trial #9						
Trial #10						

Carol found this exercise distracting. In fact, after trial number 1, Carol reported both blurry vision and dizziness. She rated it a SUDS of 83. By trial number 4, she was down to a 20 rating on the SUDS scale. This exercise made Carol laugh. "You gotta be kidding! What does this have to do with anxiety?" But after trial number 1, she felt lightheaded and dizzy. She said, "My heart skipped a beat! That was a 90." But she rated trial number 6 a 15.

Sit in a straight-backed chair and put your head between your legs. Make sure that your head is below your heart. After 1 minute, sit up straight. Like the standing-up exercise, this creates an abrupt change in the blood flow to your head, resulting in lightheadedness, blurry vision, and a little dizziness.

HEAD BETWEEN YOUR LEGS WORKSHEET

EXERCISES	DESCRIBE YOUR SYMPTOMS	SUDS	WORST FEAR	ODDS OF THIS HAPPENING	DID IT HAPPEN?	YOUR COPING SKILLS
Trial #1						
Trial #2						

Trial #3						
Trial #4						
Trial #5						
Trial #6						
Trial #7						
Trial #8						
Trial #9						
Trial #10						

These exercises should be practiced regularly, especially if you have suffered from panic attacks. Practicing rewires your brain to establish the new healthy habit.

You'll have plenty of opportunities for interoceptive exposure when you don't plan it. The physical sensations you feared can still occur spontaneously. When they do, you will probably feel a little more anxious. That's okay, and it's expected. You can now react to them as false alarms.

Consider spontaneous events as opportunities to practice your new counter-conditioning skills. You'll get better at dealing with them as you practice inducing the symptoms. The more you practice, the more prepared you'll be to derail a potential panic attack. By practicing the interoceptive exposure exercises with the techniques you have learned in the preceding chapters, your panic attacks will probably fade away.

Chapter 10
Preventing Relapse

Now that you have learned the skills to minimize anxiety, you'll want to make sure that these gains last. To ensure that they actually do last, you'll need to keep with the program. This means practicing the skills you've learned regularly.

From a brain-based perspective, repetition is critical for the neuroplasticity that rewires your brain and instills new habits. If you fall back into old patterns, you'll rekindle the old neural networks that bring back anxiety. Think of anxiety as an old habit that you want only as a distant memory. In this chapter, you'll learn how to prevent relapse into your old anxiety habit.

MINIMIZING YOUR VULNERABILITY

Several factors can influence your vulnerability to anxiety relapse. You *reduce* your vulnerability by taking care of your body and especially your brain. You *increase* it by subjecting yourself to bad habits that contribute to stress. Following are some examples of habits that can negatively affect your vulnerability to relapse:

- poor diet
- alcohol or other drugs
- not getting enough sleep
- dehydration
- experiencing interpersonal conflict
- multitasking
- cramming for exams or to complete projects
- taking on too much over a short period of time
- forgetting to pace yourself and practice

Unique stressors identified by people in my class include:

- talking to my sister
- seeing other nervous people
- smoking marijuana
- drinking a quadruple latte
- being asked my opinion
- driving in rush hour traffic

You want to minimize these factors, so that you're less vulnerable to stress and anxiety. It's unfortunately too easy to forget to take care of yourself. Don't make it a habit! Stay in shape, so that you can minimize your vulnerability.

What factors have made you vulnerable? They might include some from the list on the previous page, as well as others that are unique to you. Take a moment to write them down.

WHAT ARE YOUR STRESSORS?

_____   _____

_____   _____

_____   _____

_____   _____

Come back to this list from time to time, to remind yourself of the factors to minimize. You can also add others as they occur to you and as they come up. The overall plan is to eliminate these factors, so that you can keep your vulnerability low. The difference between eliminating factors that make you vulnerable to anxiety and avoiding situations that make you anxious is all about what's good for you. A bad diet is not good for you. Being with people, despite being anxious around people, is good for you. You want to avoid a bad diet; you don't want to avoid people.

Practice Good Self-Care

One of the clearest ways to minimize your vulnerability to anxiety symptoms is to practice good self-care. You want your brain and the rest of your body to be fit.

Consume a healthy diet.   Consuming a diet that includes too much sugar, caffeine, and unbalanced meals can promote a neurochemistry that simulates anxiety. Such a diet makes you vulnerable to inducing anxiety symptoms such as rapid heartbeat, sweating, insomnia, lightheadedness, shakiness, and shortness of breath. Remember to eat at least three balanced meals a day.

Avoid alcohol and other drugs.   Alcohol and other drugs create an imbalance in your neurochemistry that lasts for days and even weeks after your last drink. Also, the day after consuming alcohol (even though the quantity may not be great), you'll be dehydrated.

Stay adequately hydrated.   Dehydration contributes to feeling uneasy. Because you are more than 80 percent water, dehydration compromises your body, including your brain cells. When your brain cells are compromised, you're less likely to cope with stress and more likely to feel anxious.

Get enough sleep.   Sleep loss makes it more difficult to concentrate, increases your emotional liability, and decreases your ability to deal with stress. If you lose sleep, you may have symptoms such as lightheadedness, shakiness, and feeling tense.

Learn to deal with stress. Stress can destabilize your capacity to function properly, wear you down, and make you more vulnerable to developing symptoms of anxiety. Stress in itself is not a bad thing. In fact, stress is a fact of life, and you don't want to avoid tasks just because they are stressful. It's how you deal with stress that determines the degree of vulnerability to anxiety. Regular practice of coping skills, including the anxiety-reduction techniques you learned, will minimize stress and anxiety.

Avoid multitasking. As you learned earlier, making thinking errors can inadvertently promote anxiety, and you are more likely to make thinking errors if you multitask. This is because it's hard to sort out all your thoughts and feelings when you are shifting from task to task. There's a risk that your scattered thoughts and feelings can add up to feeling overwhelmed. Your thinking then shifts to globalizing—lumping everything together. Multitasking, therefore, promotes stress and then anxiety.

Multitasking includes talking on your cell phone, instant messaging, and text messaging while you are engaging in important activities. One of my concerns is that increasing numbers of people are talking on cell phones while driving, sometimes in difficult traffic. Don't do it! Multitasking like this causes accidents.

Dawn Learns to Minimize Her Multitasking

Dawn came to see me after rear-ending a car at a stop light. She had been talking on her cell phone while driving. Fortunately, the collision caused no injuries, but it certainly did cause a jump in her insurance premiums and her anxiety. After attending the anxiety class for several weeks, she said she had learned a lot, but that she couldn't give up one bad habit. Although she hated to admit it, she was addicted to multitasking. She rationalized it by saying, "I can get more done than most people." I reminded her of the accident, and she agreed to stop using her cell phone while driving.

Dawn's problems resurfaced when she hit a snag with one of her tasks and tumbled into a panic attack. Instead of shifting her attention solely to the problem that needed resolving, she continued to try and juggle all the balls at once. When I noted that all the balls that she had been juggling seemed to bounce off her head, she said, "I know! I hate it when that happens!" She acknowledged that it was time to develop a contingency strategy. Although she was unwilling to give up multitasking entirely, she did agree that when she ran into a problem with one of her tasks, she would postpone her involvement on the others until the snag was worked through. This contingency strategy helped derail a panic attack before it happened.

Label the cause of your anxiety. When you begin to feel the symptoms of anxiety, it is helpful to label the cause of it. Dawn, for example, learned to shift from multitasking to completing one task at a time. By labeling her experience, she was able to maintain a realistic perspective on work and lessen her anxiety. When she ran into difficulty with one of her tasks and found herself becoming anxious, she said, "I'm getting those panic feelings again, because I can't juggle this all right now. I need to get back to doing one thing at a time." Just saying this to herself lowered her anxiety level. Then she followed through with our plan to resolve one task before returning her attention to the others.

Labeling puts things in perspective and helps derail movement to a panic attack. It helps a lot to simply say to yourself, "I've just had a very upsetting argument." Labeling keeps you from lumping all your thoughts and feelings into an overwhelming and unmanageable globalized catastrophe. Labeling also activates your left frontal lobe and helps you shift away from overactivating your right frontal lobe. Remember that your left frontal lobe processes positive (can-do) emotions, and your right frontal lobe processes negative (anxious) emotions.

Seek social support.   Humans are social creatures, so getting support from your close friends and relatives and a partner or spouse can be a great antidote to stress and anxiety. When those relationships are thrown into doubt, such as after a major argument, you can be more vulnerable to experiencing a relapse of anxiety. If you can't resolve the situation with the person, seek out social support from close friends or your spouse to buffer the residual effects of the conflict.

RECOGNIZING YOUR ANXIETY TRIGGERS

You can minimize your vulnerability to anxiety, but various situations that triggered anxiety in the past, such as being in a rainstorm or having trouble in a relationship, can occur again. The road to recovery is littered with obstacles, bumps, and chuckholes in the form of stressful situations that can trigger anxiety. This means that setbacks can occur.

Your challenge is to see these setbacks as mere bumps on the road. When you are driving down a road and your car hits a chuckhole, you don't pull over and say to yourself, "I can't do this! The road is too rough!" You simply acknowledge that there are chuckholes and adjust your speed accordingly.

When you hold on to avoidant behaviors (such as avoiding driving because of chuckholes), you increase the likelihood of relapse. Relapse prevention should include continual real-life exposure to habituate you to situations you fear. Expose yourself to the situation in which the fear originated. By making repeated exposures to the initial fear-provoking situation, you can form new associations to it. Also, you can develop positive self-talk to disprove your anxiety-provoking predictions of danger.

Anna Develops New Associations

Anna developed free-floating anxiety with periodic panic attacks after being harassed at work. She filed a grievance, then quit. Although she found another job, her anxiety and panic attacks continued. She was later referred to my anxiety class and experienced relief from her anxiety relatively quickly. However, she still avoided driving on the road near her previous place of employment. In fact, she went out of her way to avoid it. We developed an exposure plan to get her back on the road. By using anxiety-reduction techniques and developing a different association to the road, Anna eventually was able to drive on it. The new associations were formed by having her stop at a grocery store located on the road. We agreed that she would actually go out of her way to get to that store to shop, so that she could recondition herself. Even after she developed a new association to the road, she periodically shopped at the store near her former place of employment, "just to stay in practice."

As you develop your relapse plan, keep in mind the context in which your anxiety is prone to occur. Think of the context as filled with cues that trigger your anxious reactions. Anxiety cues are like signals that alert you that something dangerous is coming. The problem is that many are false alarms. Katie, for example, had a tendency to feel intimidated by people who expressed thought-provoking opinions and reacted by being overwhelmed with anxiety. Those types of people became the cues that triggered her anxiety. Through work in my class, she learned to convert these cues into a positive. Instead of responding with anxiety, she now responds with curiosity and seeks them out to hear their opinions.

What unique cues trigger your anxiety? Use the worksheet below to note the cues that trigger your anxiety, the symptoms that develop, your SUDS score, the old coping skills that you used, the skills you forgot to use, and the plan to modify your coping techniques. I filled in the first block with Katie's responses, as an example. Jot down your unique details and give a lot of thought to what coping skills you forgot and your planning for next time.

CUES PLANNING WORKSHEET

CUES	SYMPTOMS	SUDS	OLD COPING SKILLS	WHAT I FORGOT TO DO	MY PLANNING
intimidatir	sweating	85	leaving if an	stay in the room	stay in the room
people	palms and		intimidating	and practice my	and ask the person
	feeling		person entered	breathing and	a question about
	shaky		the room	positive self-talk	her opinion

Sometimes the cues that trigger anxiety are unanticipated. They aren't as easily planned for, and they take you by surprise. How can you plan for the unexpected? You can't know the future, but you can realistically estimate situations that are truly dangerous when they do occur. This can be a balancing act, because you had a tendency in the past to overestimate danger. Here's what to do:

1. If you're still avoiding specific situations because you "feel" anxious about them but don't have any realistic evidence that the situations are dangerous, use exposure and avoid avoidance.

2. As situations come up, use realistic measures to assess for true danger, including whether most people would find the situation dangerous or unbearable.

3. If you estimate that a situation is not dangerous but merely anxiety-provoking, begin graduated exposures.

4. Remember that exposure is your method of neutralizing anxiety-provoking experiences. As you identify remaining "hot spots," attack them with exposure. Much like a firefighter identifies hot spots and puts them out, instead of avoiding them, your job is to search out your own hot spots and put them out through exposure.

Brenda Converts an Anxiety Cue into an Opportunity

Brenda learned to put out hot spots as part of her long-term relapse plan. A community college instructor, she made great gains in the anxiety class. One of Brenda's hot spots was dealing with students who seemed critical of what was going on in class. She feared talking to them because she worried that it would be like opening Pandora's Box—she assumed she would hear personal criticism. She assumed that it was best to let well enough alone. When she encountered a student who seemed critical, she would respond by becoming anxious. I suggested she approach the student during break or after class and simply ask: "Is there anything I can help you out with?" If the student rebuffed her, she could say, "I just want you to know that if you're having any difficulty, I can help." By approaching the student in this way, she was able to make an ally out of him by demonstrating her concerns within a positive context. She converted an anxiety cue into an opportunity.

It's critical to avoid avoidance behaviors and to expose yourself consistently to those remaining anxiety-provoking cues, so that they no longer trigger anxiety. Your long-term plan must entail consistent exposure to the context of the cues that you were avoiding. By exposing yourself to these cues long after your anxiety has faded, you can continue to habituate to them, and you'll engender a sense of durability that can help you when you encounter these cues in the future. This is because the cues that provoke anxiety will become a mere memory. They don't trigger anxiety anymore, because you have made them innocuous. When you continue to expose yourself to them, you keep them converted.

The conversion of cues that trigger anxiety to simple memories provides a vantage point from which you can recognize that many cues and anxiety triggers are arbitrary. Many were associated with anxiety only in your mind. Those cues can as easily be associated with neutral, or even positive, feelings. Your job is to identify those cues and convert them into neutral or positive feelings. This conversion can only be accomplished by continual exposure.

MANAGING SETBACKS

It's quite common to experience brief periods of anxiety during and after the recovery process. Almost no one is anxiety-free. This is because anxiety is a good thing. The question is how much you have and how overwhelming it is for you. Your anxiety was not useful to you in the past, and your job now is to make it normal.

Unfortunately, it's quite common for people to get so excited about their progress that they gravitate back to all-or-nothing thinking. Fueled by enthusiasm, they assume that they have been "cured" and that they are completely anxiety-free. Once they've made this thinking error, they're at risk of experiencing minor setbacks with periods of disturbing anxiety and falling back into their old pattern of overreacting to the anxiety. What was once a little anxiety becomes a great deal of anxiety. They assume that they are back to square one, that all the progress they made is lost, and that they have to start all over again. Worse, some people think of themselves as incapable of making *any* long-term progress.

Following are some of the common overreactions to setbacks:

- "Why try if I'm just going to fall back again?"
- "After all the work I've done, I'm right back where I started from."
- "I knew I was incapable of making it last."
- "This must mean that my anxiety problem is worse than I thought."
- "Maybe I should go back to avoiding things that make me anxious."
- "I guess the gains I made were all superficial."
- "All those anxiety-reduction techniques weren't for people with deep problems like mine."
- "I can't change my anxiety genes."
- "Everything I've done is lost now, and I can't climb back up."
- "All those techniques were just distractions from my real problem."
- "I might as well just go on medication."

Unique thinking error responses to minor setbacks from people in my anxiety class include:

- "My mother taught me how to be anxious all the time. I guess I should expect it."
- "I've got a rare anxiety condition and will never be free of terrible anxiety."
- "Medical marijuana is the answer."
- "This relapse proves I've got bad brain chemistry."
- "I guess I've got brain damage, after all."
- "God forgets to help me sometimes."

Setbacks are opportunities to learn lessons. They remind you that you weren't practicing your coping skills and that there's still work to be done. They let you know that you have not been following the plan. Following are some realistic responses to a setback:

- "I guess I was forgetting to take care of myself."
- "I better practice my coping techniques more often."
- "I was getting too lazy."
- "Whoops. I let myself get out of shape."
- "That was a good reminder to stay with my plan."
- "I should see one task through, rather than lumping everything together."
- "There's something to learn from this."

Following are some unique responses from people in my class.

- "Nobody said it would be easy."
- "I'll hang in there long term because of my kids."
- "It's like I'm training for a long-distance run. I'll pace myself."
- "I do too much for other people and not enough for myself."
- "I'm going to find my groove again."
- "Time to get back into balance once again."
- "I will reinstall the shock absorbers."
- "Time to snap out of that fear jag."
- "My anxiety habit took years to develop, it'll take a while to unlearn."
- "I'm not a computer that can be instantaneously reprogrammed."

Worrying is a slippery slope for other types of anxiety. Perhaps you started worrying about meeting new people once again. Then you did everything you could to keep from interacting with them, to reduce your anxiety. You forgot that exposure is the antidote, it's like an inoculation. To both neutralize the worrying and prevent a setback, be sure to apply exposure.

Regardless of the factors that contribute to a setback, your task is to learn from the experience, so that the setback can be worthwhile. Yes, worthwhile. Think of the setbacks as an opportunity to move ahead, rather than look back and lament.

You may have already had a setback. What did you tell yourself? What did you learn from the setback? What made you vulnerable, and what did you do to become less vulnerable to future setbacks?

HOW DO YOU DEAL WITH SETBACKS?

_____   _____

_____   _____

_____   _____

_____   _____

_____   _____

_____   _____

_____   _____

Examine your setbacks, so that you can learn how you reverted to your old habits. Develop a plan that includes:

- Keeping yourself from overreacting to your physical symptoms through interoceptive exposure.
- Observing the sensations, instead of overreacting and seeing them as a call for alarm and eventual panic.
- Keeping yourself from doing too many things at once and worrying about them all at once.
- Dealing with each situation independently by chunking your tasks.
- Keeping yourself from becoming too tired or hungry.
- Pacing yourself, so you don't feel pressured to complete a task too quickly.

INTEGRATING RELAPSE-PREVENTION SKILLS INTO YOUR EVERYDAY LIFE

Over the course of this book, you have courageously engaged in many exercises that have challenged you to do things that didn't "feel right." You should congratulate yourself for these efforts. Your relapse-prevention plan should involve integrating all that you have learned into long-term practice. Remind yourself of your accomplishments to maintain your new perspective and to remind yourself that you are capable of meeting challenges that once seemed insurmountable. Maybe you thought you could never fly on an airplane or talk in front of a group of people.

No one technique alone is sufficient for your long-term relapse-prevention plan. A durable plan includes all the techniques together. Relying on one or just a few techniques is like your car running on just a few pistons. There are a number of things that you need to practice, so that your relapse prevention plan is integrated:

Breathing: Practice regular abdominal breathing.

Good dietary habits: Be sure to properly fuel your brain.

Good sleep habits: Be sure to get enough sleep.

Social support: Seek out the support of friends and family.

Focusing: Be here now. By focusing on the here and now, you shift your attention away from anxiously predicting the future.

Avoiding avoidance behaviors: Expose yourself to life.

Being assertive: Stay away from passivity.

Learning Assertiveness

Assertiveness shifts you from passivity to approach behaviors, which activate your left frontal lobe and its positive emotions. Recall from chapter 3 that over-activating your right frontal lobe induces passivity and anxiety. Being assertive allows you to meet challenges by confronting them head-on, instead of reacting to them in a passive, defensive way, always bracing yourself for the next onslaught of stress and anxiety. Being assertive can mean different things for different people. If you're shy, for example, being socially assertive will be harder than it would be for people who aren't shy. This doesn't mean that you get a free pass from making an effort socially. Your goal might not include becoming the life of the party, but you certainly can learn to be more assertive than you are right now.

By being assertive, you're in the driver's seat of your own life, instead of the passenger seat. You decide where to go and what you want to do, instead of reacting to what occurs. Here's where your frontal lobes can have control over the reactivity of your amygdala. And here's where your action-oriented left frontal lobe balances out the passive right frontal lobe. Along with this shift to your left frontal lobe comes its positive emotions, instead of the negative emotions associated with the right frontal lobe.

Mara Gains Confidence Through Assertiveness

Mara came to my class after experiencing an increase in panic attacks. She had suffered attacks in her late adolescence, but they faded away rather quickly. Recently, she had taken a new job with a supervisor who did not value his employees. Simultaneously, she went through a rough time with her boyfriend. He, too, was experiencing stress, but his method of dealing with it was to dump it on her.

Mara's panic attacks reemerged after arguments with him and then increased in intensity over the following weeks. After being in the anxiety class for five sessions, she practiced all the skills that you learned in this book. She enjoyed a reduction in her symptoms and was delighted to see her panic attacks fade away.

Soon thereafter she stopped coming to the class. Unfortunately, she left before we covered relapse prevention. Two weeks after leaving, she returned to the class concerned that she had "gone back to square one." She had had a series of panic attacks after she and her boyfriend had more fights and now feared that she had lost all the gains she had made.

I explained that setbacks are common, especially if relapse-prevention skills are not practiced on a regular basis. She admitted to assuming that she was cured and had completely conquered anxiety and so stopped practicing her coping skills. She ignored her diet and stopped practicing breathing exercises. By the time she and her boyfriend had their latest fight, she was already feeling free-floating anxiety.

I used Mara's return to the class as an opportunity to reemphasize the methods of relapse prevention. With Mara in mind, we covered the importance of assertiveness. She had become far too passive in her life. This was especially true in her relationship with her boyfriend. She tended to spoil him, and he took advantage of the opportunity to assume the role of the most important person in their relationship.

Learning to be assertive with her boyfriend wasn't easy. He didn't like that Mara was changing. However, when he said, "you've changed," she thanked him for the compliment. Of course, she knew that he was really complaining. She continued to develop assertiveness by telling him that her "change" would be permanent and that she would no longer sacrifice her needs to take care of him. Mara also practiced assertiveness at work. She and her coworkers began to discuss common purposes and cultivated mutual respect with the supervisors.

Mara began to feel confident again. But, this time, she didn't slack off on her relapse-prevention plan. Although she did experience some bumps along the way, with occasional periods of anxiety, she put things into perspective, and, with the use of her coping skills, those bumps drifted by as inconsequential.

Rate Your Skill Strength
Staying in shape means practicing all the techniques on a regular basis. The more you practice them, the more they will become second nature to you. They will become the new habits that replace your old anxiety habits.

At this point, you'll want to determine what part of the full repertoire of practices you have been weakest in developing, so that you can shore that up. Use the following worksheet to rate where you are strong and where you are weak. Rank them by assigning a number #1 for the strongest and so on. Also write down your plan to improve that skill.

SKILLS CHECKUP WORKSHEET

SKILL	RANK	PLAN TO IMPROVE IT

After you complete the worksheet on the opposite page, note the skills you ranked the lowest. I want you to make those your strongest skills. Your first response might be: "Why not stay with the ones I like the best?" or possibly, "What I've done already is good enough!"

You want to increase your durability as part of your relapse-prevention plan. To promote durability, you'll need to shore up your weak areas by practicing them more often and not rely solely on your strong suits. Consider this: You're only as strong as your weakest link. If you transform your weakest links into your strongest, your current strongest will be your weakest.

While you're strengthening yourself, you need to take care of yourself at the same time. Self-soothing behaviors involve doing not only things that help you relax but also things that excite and activate you. If you fall into a mode of always trying to relax, you'll relapse by developing anxiety sensitivity. You'll be so focused on reducing anxiety that any anxiety will feel like too much.

You need a balance between activation and relaxation, between your sympathetic and parasympathetic nervous systems. Your sympathetic nervous system gets you activated. It helps you get excited about positive things, such as watching a good movie, playing your favorite sport, or embarking on an adventure. Positive things bring a rush of excitement and activate the neuro-transmitters dopamine, norepinephrine, and epinephrine (adrenaline).

Your parasympathetic nervous system helps calm you down. If you focus too much on one system and avoid the other, you can set yourself up for an imbalanced life and a relapse of anxiety. You need both excitement and relaxation to keep your life varied, enjoyable, and balanced. Self-soothing, therefore, involves excitement as well as relaxation.

Remember that the way you perceive your symptoms or any given situation can either stoke up anxiety or help you cope with the situation. Include developing positive meaning for each experience in your relapse-prevention plan. The meaning is framed by your automatic thoughts, assumptions, and core beliefs. Relapse prevention is strengthened by the consistent positive and constructive meaning that you give to your experiences.

Michelle Shifts to a Constructive Belief

Michelle had a tendency to view the world as a hostile place, until she came to the anxiety class. She grew up in a hostile neighborhood in South Central Los Angeles, where gang slayings were not uncommon. Although she was fortunate to earn a scholarship to go away to college, she had a hard time easing up to trust people at school. Years later, after suffering periods of anxiety punctuated by panic attacks, she came in for help. The class helped her change her belief system. She worked to shed her hypervigilance about who she could trust and began cultivating the skills to apply positive meaning to her experiences.

In the sixth week of attending the class, she reported that a rift had developed between her colleagues at work. Her coworkers were taking sides, almost like rival gangs, and she felt they were asking her to choose one over the other. Images of gang rivalry in her old neighborhood engulfed her. Through coaching in the class, she was able to shift to a constructive belief that the rift was beneath her and that she could focus on the higher common denominator between the opposing groups of people. She refused to come down to their level of winners and losers. She told those trying to recruit her that she would be glad to help them find common ground with those that they opposed. As she took the high road without alienating herself from personal relationships with her peers, her anxiety subsided.

Setting Guidelines for Relapse Prevention

1. **Relish challenges.** One of the most positive core beliefs you can embrace is to relish challenges. The hunger for challenge can be vitalizing. Your ability to stay flexible and assign positive meaning to all your experiences will be critical for facing challenges. Consider each new experience a manageable challenge that is within your capacity to meet. Your thinking should promote optimism and the belief that you are up to most challenges.

2. **Soothe yourself.** Be prepared to soothe yourself as you encounter stress or periods of anxiety in the face of difficult situations. This can go a long way toward making a stressful situation tolerable. Self-soothing does not involve babying yourself. It simply means that you help yourself feel at ease during stress by using the relaxation skills that you've learned: breathing, positive self-talk, imagery, and self-hypnosis. Mindfulness will be especially useful to help you focus your attention and relax at the same time.

3. **Regulate your emotions.** Being able to regulate your emotions does not mean tightly controlling them. You learned that rigid efforts to stamp out any semblance of anxiety leads to more anxiety. Success in regulating your emotions involves letting go of the compulsion to control them. You can promote positive emotions by doing things that make you feel good and relaxed. If you are intensely focused on a particularly challenging task, incorporate your coping techniques, while challenging yourself to lean into that task.

4. **Make anxiety your friend.** Remember that a little anxiety is expected and perfectly normal. Your success is based on your ability to manage and orchestrate anxiety to make it work for you. Make anxiety your friend. Don't run away from it. This means that you must eliminate avoidance behaviors. Resist reverting back to old avoidant behaviors by telling yourself, "I've been good pushing myself, and now I need a break from all this exposure stuff."

5. **Eliminate safety behaviors.** As you remember from the chapter on exposure, even safety behaviors are fool's gold. On the surface, they appear to be good ways to decrease anxiety, but they actually contribute to anxiety. Therefore, you want your relapse-prevention plan to eliminate safety behaviors. Don't give yourself an easy way out because you fear encountering some anxiety.

6. **Stick with your exposure exercises.** Consider them long-term treatments for anxiety. You need a "maintenance dose" of exposure exercises over the long term to keep yourself habituated to the experiences that you once found anxiety-provoking. Regular exposure is the way to stay "in condition."

7. **Seek out social support.** Social support is a critical part of your relapse-prevention plan. Because you are human, key parts of your brain thrive on social contact. You'll need these systems fully activated. As I described in chapter 3, these systems comprise what has been called the "social brain." They were very much involved in your early bonding experiences with your parents. These regions of your brain, which include your orbital frontal cortex, are highly involved in the regulation of emotion. When you activate your social brain, you also activate the parts of your brain that regulate your emotions. You do this by maintaining your social support system.

Withdrawing from your social support system deactivates your social brain. Your orbital frontal cortex will then be less useful in regulating your emotions. Even though you might not feel like being with people when you are anxious, social contact is still good for you. Think of it as "social medicine." Make sure that you relapse prevention plan includes a regular dose of social medicine.

Pete Learns the Importance of Social Medicine

An IT specialist in a huge law firm, Pete's job was to fix the firm's computer and network systems. Working in the office were more than fifty lawyers and seventy support personnel, who at times made Pete feel intimidated. He managed to keep himself insulated from social contact by minimizing small talk to focus solely on the computer systems. He had only one friend in the office, another IT person. Unfortunately, because much of the firm's work centered around real estate law, during the mortgage home loan bust, 20 percent of the office staff was laid off, including Pete's friend. His work load doubled, as did his anxiety level.

Always a worrier, Pete's anxiety was spurred to new heights. He found himself extremely sensitive to even an inkling of displeasure from the staff members. Because he had no friends to bounce things off of, those worries were like runaway trains. That's when he came to see me. Initially, he resisted coming to the class because he felt he wasn't good with people. "Why would you want me to do anything that is going to make my condition worse?" I explained that in addition to learning how to deal with anxiety, he would have an opportunity to practice social skills.

Pete's first few weeks in the class helped him rein in his anxiety and dampen some of his worrying. But he was quiet and only spoke to me after the class, once the others had gone. It was obvious that he wanted social contact, because he stayed after the class and seemed to want to make small talk. I convinced him to arrive early and practice talking to his peers. I stressed that it was important for his long-term relapse-prevention plan to develop these small-talk skills at work. Expanding on these skills was important for his social medicine.

He dropped out of the class after about two months, explaining that he'd gotten what he needed. Three months later he returned, complaining that he had relapsed. He had continued with all of the anxiety reduction skills but the social medicine. He said that he "got lazy," and it was "too much work" to make an effort socially. He essentially fell back into his comfort zone.

Pete's anxiety level spiked when the firm hit yet another financial crisis and more people were laid off. Staff members were getting irritable, and, when their computers broke down, they sometimes took their frustration out on him. Because Pete's relationships with many of them were dormant, he had no one to talk to, and his worrying once again intensified.

His return to class presented an opportunity to emphasize how important social medicine is to a relapse-prevention plan. He began to practice his small-talk skills with peers, and soon the small talk became the gateway to deeper conversations. His desire for friendships spilled over into work. During the next financial crisis at work, the social medicine aspect of his relapse-prevention plan helped provide shock absorbers for the bumpy ride.

Creating Your Relapse-Prevention Plan

Your relapse-prevention plan should include many facets. Use the worksheet on p. 175 to make sure that you adhere to each facet. As you continue to work on your relapse-prevention plan, remember that life itself is a challenge. And that's a good thing! Challenges make life interesting, exciting, and eventful. Face your challenges head-on, so that you can feel proud of yourself. Embrace those challenges, and, as a consequence, your anxiety will fade away.

In the date section of the worksheet, write down the date each week, to ensure that you are staying on top of each facet. Use the blank spaces in the Domain column to write in specific parts of your unique monitoring plan. For example, if going to church or doing yoga is part of it, write it down. The important thing is to monitor all the facets of your plan, so that you don't leave anything out.

RELAPSE-PREVENTION MONITORING WORKSHEET

DOMAIN	DATE	DATE	DATE	DATE	DATE	DATE	DATE	DATE	DATE	DATE
Diet										
Breathing										
Thinking Skills										
Exposures										
Social Medicine										
Interoceptive Exposure										
Relaxation Skills										

About the Author

John B. Arden, Ph.D., is the Director of Training for the Northern California region in mental health for the Kaiser Permanente Medical Centers. In this capacity, he oversees one of the largest mental health training programs in the world, which trains 64 postdoctoral psychology residents and 50 interns per year. During his 38 years of experience in the mental health field, he has worked as a psychologist, chief psychologist, and training director, and he has taught in universities and colleges.

He has been fortunate to work in a system that has researched and offered the very latest treatment modalities for anxiety. This book is based on his work with people who have anxiety disorders. Part of this work has centered on teaching a class for people with anxiety disorders, and much of the information contained in the book reflects the lessons that been found to be instrumentative in helping people overcome anxiety.

He is the author or coauthor of 13 other books, including *Rewire Your Brain, The Brain Bible, Conquering Post-Traumatic Stress Disorder, Brain-Based Therapy—Adults,* and *Brain-Based Therapy—Child.* John lives in Northern California.

Made in the USA
Monee, IL
16 November 2020

47941553R00077